# Moral Change

Cecilie Eriksen

# Moral Change

## Dynamics, Structure, and Normativity

palgrave
macmillan

Cecilie Eriksen
Utrecht University
Utrecht, The Netherlands

ISBN 978-3-030-61036-4 ISBN 978-3-030-61037-1 (eBook)
https://doi.org/10.1007/978-3-030-61037-1



This Palgrave Macmillan imprint is published by the registered company Springer Nature Switzerland AG.
The registered company address is: Gewerbestrasse 11, 6330 Cham, Switzerland

Dedicated to my parents, Bjarne and Lise.

# Preface

> Yet to admit the dying of knowledge, as to endure the dying of love, as to succumb to the death of God and of poetry, may be all that fits one for rebirth. (Cavell 1999: 449)

This started out as a curiosity quest and ended as a book of betrayal. An old fascination with Nietzsche's call to 'move beyond good and evil' turned into speculations on what actually does lead to moral changes—and how, if the values of his own society were rotten and infected with an unhealthy form of religion, did Nietzsche find the resources to ethically criticize them?

In the following philosophical investigations of moral change, I attempt to pay justice to several different aspects of the ethical, which are all essential, but difficult to balance and hold together in one outlook on life. These are aspects like change and continuity, human dependency and human freedom, what is common to humans and different between people and peoples, the immanent and the transcending aspect of morality as well as the ethical as being *sui generis* (i.e. not being reducible to, e.g. the social, legal, political, economic and biological) and potentially related to all other aspects of the weave of human life. The two aspects, which have haunted me the most in this regard, are what I term 'moral certainty' and 'moral uncertainty'. The relationship between these two phenomena is not symmetric. Moral certainty is the far more prevailing phenomenon in human life. This is important to show and pay respect to, because if it was not human life would wither and disappear. Nonetheless, even though moral certainty is the more prevailing phenomenon, moral uncertainty—doubts, insecurities, indeterminacies—is from an ethical point of view equally important to pay justice to. For that reason—that moral certainty is the more prevailing phenomenon—the best metaphor for understanding the flaws in this book is not, I believe, as a lack of balance between the two scales in Lady Justitia's hand. In that image the scale of certainty should be the heavier. My betrayal is rather that I did not find a way of writing about moral certainty and uncertainty, which allows them both to be alive in the text simultaneously. Often, when I describe and call attention to moral certainty in human life, it leaves me with an unsettling sense of betraying the openness of morality; that, for instance, I and we could be acting unjustly, unloving, irresponsible despite adhering to our moral ideals. The text turns moralistic, at times even dogmatic. And whenever I write about moral uncertainty, I feel I betray phenomena like the joy, cruelty, care, injustice and love which we encounter in our lives. If I were to doubt or question the suffering of a survivor of the genocide against the Tutsi or the love my brother has for me, it would not only be indecent, but 'something holy would be profaned'.

Perhaps a better metaphor for the balance I struggle with in this work is that of the high-wire artist, who, in order to keep the balance while moving forward, has to adjust her body from one side to the other, slowly up and down, small movements in all directions. I know I from time to time thought of the mad courage and elegant beauty of Philippe Petit walking between the Twin Towers, while writing. And I occasionally dreamt of falling, failing, forgetting the unforgettable during the nights. I found hope, though, in the words of a scruffy poster, I once saw hanging on the wall of a workshop: "Everything in its right place provides space for everything". My job was to keep on trying.

The following people deserve heartfelt thanks for the help they have given during the many years this book has been underway. I would first of all like to thank Anne-Marie Søndergaard Christensen for years of productive co-work, fun and encouragement. I would like to thank Sten Schaumburg-Müller for crucial help in starting this project, and I would like to thank Jens Vedsted-Hansen and Ingrid Ravn for friendly guidance in foggy times. A special thanks is owed to Maria Louw, Rasmus Dyring, Lotte Meinert, Thomas W. Schwartz, Lone Grøn, Martijn van Beek and Marie Rask Bjerre Odgaard, all members of, first, the reading group *PARG* and then later the research project *Ethics after individualism*—the best philosophical–anthropological playgrounds I ever visited! A warm thanks to Joel Robbins and James Laidlaw at the Department of Social Anthropology, University of Cambridge, for housing me in spring 2019 and thus giving me an inspiring and beautiful space for finishing the book manuscript. I also owe Hans Fink, Sylvie Delacroix, Jonathan Lear, Tony Søndergaard, Bjarke Viskum, Per Andersen, Neil O'Hara and the two anonymous reviewers thanks for various forms of valuable feedback on the manuscript. I am most grateful of all for my two girls, Lovis and Lærke, who bring joy and balance to life, and for the rest of my family, David, Asger, Iris, Bjarne and Lise. I would never have made it without your love, support and help. Thank you.

Cambridge, UK
June 2019

Cecilie Eriksen

## Reference

Cavell, S. 1999. *The Claim of Reason: Wittgenstein, Scepticism, Morality and Tragedy*. Oxford University Press.

# Notes from the Author

Parts of the Introduction and Part I originally appeared in "The Dynamics of Moral Revolutions – Prelude to Future Investigations and Interventions". *Ethical Theory and Moral Practice 22* (3): 779–792 (2019). Reprinted with the permission of Springer Nature.

Parts of the chapter 'Conclusion: Army of metaphors' originally appeared in "Winds of Change: The Later Wittgenstein's Conception of the Dynamics of Change". *Nordic Wittgenstein Review, 9* (2020). Reprinted with the permission of *NWR*, de Gruyter.

Parts of the chapter 'Conclusion: Contextual ethics' appear in "Contextual ethics—taking the lead from Wittgenstein and Løgstrup on ethical meaning and normativity" in *Sats—Special Issue on Contextual Ethics* (forthcoming). Reprinted with the permission of *Sats*, de Gruyter.

The research in this book was supported by Aarhus University, School of Business and Social Sciences (case nr. 10765) and the Independent Research Fund Denmark | Culture and Communication (case nr. 7013-00068B).

# Contents

CHAPTER 1

# Introduction

By cosmic rule, as day yields night, so winter summer, war peace, plenty famine. All things change. (Heraclitus 2003: Fragment 36)

Change is one of the most striking features of morality. More than 2000 years after Heraclitus formulated his thoughts on the fundamental law of cosmos and human life, his words are echoed in the *Manifesto of the Communist Party*: "All that is solid melts into air, all that is holy is profaned" (Marx and Engels 1888: 6). This quote captures the nature of moral change as a two-edged sword. It is a source of both fear and hope. Change can destroy what we care about and hold sacred, and it can be the herald of hope for the downfall of ruthless tyrants and empty gods. It can clear the ground for a better life. It is undoubtedly the latter meaning Marx and Engels had in mind. They saw the holy of their time as a means of sedating the poor and working classes, so they did not rise against those in power to change the basic structures of society, which were harming them gravely. Marx and Engels were in other words criticising and asking for an overturn of what their society *called* good in order to be true to what *is* good.

When someone, like Marx and Engels, like Singer, like Yousafzai, like Thunberg, is criticising the values and ideals of their society, how can that be done? What leads to the overthrow or gradual change of moral beliefs,


C. Eriksen, *Moral Change*,
https://doi.org/10.1007/978-3-030-61037-1_1

ideals and values? Why, in Scandinavia, for instance, did it cease to be a father's moral duty to chastise his children, when they misbehaved? What made feuds in most of Europe stop being ethically and legally permitted? On what grounds did the demand for legal equality for homosexuals arise in parts of the Western world? In other words: What can we learn about morality by exploring moral changes, and how are we to understand the dynamics, structure and normativity of moral change? These are the central questions of this book, and its aim is to give a philosophical account of moral change.[1]

Moral change, however, is not only an intellectually fascinating phenomenon. It also raises moral worries directed at ethical normativity: When once it was considered natural that some humans were slaves, when once it was proof of a woman's innocence in the accusation of being a witch that she drowned, when thrown into a lake with her hands and legs bound, and when the colour of a person's skin has been and continues to be a reason for how just or unjust that person is treated, how can we then trust our current moral beliefs and practices? On what grounds can we allow ourselves to judge and act, if all we have at our disposal are the criteria and measuring rods of such fluid and most likely ethically flawed practices? To understand the nature of moral change and address moral worries and sceptical challenges to ethical normativity is important for several reasons. One reason lies in the importance of hope for human life. Humans need to believe that it is possible to make a positive difference in their lives and in the world in order to have the courage and stamina to act, both individually and collectively (Moody-Adams 2017: 1). It is such hope and courage to act, and act politically, that the moral and sceptical worries can threaten to undermine, if they are not addressed. This book is therefore also an investigation into hope.

It is further important to address the moral worries because democracies, their leaders and their citizens have to strike a balance between, on the one hand, mastering a respectful political, cultural, moral and religious pluralism and, on the other hand, mastering legitimate critique of

[1] The words 'ethics' and 'morality' are used synonymously in this work. There is thus not assumed any first- and second-order relationship between them, as sometimes is the case, where, for example, 'ethics' refers to what is universal and 'morality' to a certain society's conception of what is morally good and bad (or vice versa), or where 'ethics' is broad consideration over 'the good life' and 'morality' refers to 'a system of rules for what we owe to each other' (see, e.g. Løgstrup 2020; Williams 2011; Keane 2016a; Fink 2012, forthcoming).

different political, cultural, moral and religious beliefs, traditions and practices. Another way of expressing this is that a healthy democracy—in order to both be and survive *as* a democracy—needs to avoid dogmatic fundamentalism (insisting there is only one true morality, ideology and form of life) and cynical, laissez-faire subjectivism (allowing 'might to be right' or that 'anything goes'). It is a balance that is hard to find, and which is often challenged in a globalised world where various forms of transnational and international politics, trade, migrations, corporations and conflicts take place. In a democratic society it is also important that we are able to justify, also often morally, the laws we pass, the institutions we create and some of the judgements and decisions we make, because our governments and legal systems are not self-justified or morally guaranteed by a God demanding blind obedience. The legitimacy of such a society's institutions arises from being of service to, not only *the* people, but people. Therefore, it is important to discuss how we can steer clear of both dogmatic fundamentalism and cynical subjectivism.

The belief that it is possible to avoid subjectivism in questions of how we should live is at odds with what Jaeggi argues is a dominant trend in philosophy since Rawls and Habermas, namely that the ethical content of forms of life cannot be criticised or deemed better than other forms of life, because in modern societies there is an irreducible and incommensurable ethical pluralism (Jaeggi 2018: ix):

> Philosophy has thus withdrawn from the Socratic [...] question of how we [are to] lead our lives [and this question] has been consigned to the domain of unquestioned preferences or irreducible and unchallengeable identities. As with taste, there is no quarrelling with forms of life. (Jaeggi 2005: 65)

This book belongs to another, equally influential trend in current philosophy, that has, for example, Nussbaum as one of its prominent voices, which argues that there is an irreducible pluralism of forms of life, but these are not, or, as I will argue, at least not fully, incommensurable. Sometimes we do succeed with ethically and politically fruitful debates, critiques and quarrels over forms of life. I thus share Eldridge's intuition that:

> it is at least plausible to suppose that there may be a middle way between dogmatic appeals to sources of value that are independent of human life, on the one hand, and taking human life to be nothing but a matter of

unconstrained competition for purely subjective satisfactions, on the other. (Eldridge 2016: 15)

The investigation undertaken in this book is philosophical, and accordingly, the methods applied are philosophical. The understanding of philosophy underlying it—its theoretical frame—is Wittgensteinian (Wittgenstein 2009: §§89–133; Kuusela 2008).[2] This choice of frame is made because Wittgenstein's later work displays great sensitivity to the fluid and contingent traits of human life and their consequences for normative and epistemological issues. The conception of normativity found in his work further manages to avoid both dogmatic foundationalism and subjectivism and relativism (Stern 2003: 201; Crary 2007b; Kuusela 2008: 95–286). I have also taken my initial methodological lead from Wittgenstein's advice, delivered in the form of a straight order: "Don't think, but look!" (Wittgenstein 2009: § 66). When we seek philosophical understanding of a phenomenon, some of Wittgenstein's methodological suggestions are to think of how we learned the word for the phenomenon, to remind ourselves how this word is used in everyday talk, and investigate and describe the language-games we have for it (Wittgenstein 2009: §§ 23, 43, 77, 486).[3] As the latter suggestion makes clear, philosophical investigations are not investigations into 'mere words', but into human

[2] Philosophical method is not one individual, distinct method, but the use of a large variety of approaches and tools (see, e.g. Baggini and Fosl 2010; Haug 2017). The choice of specific methods depends among other things on which problem one is addressing and on one's conception of philosophy: what philosophy is and aims for. There is no general agreement in philosophy as to how 'philosophy' should be defined and understood (Daly 2010: 9–13; Hämäläinen 2016: 7–8). Unsurprisingly, there is also no general agreement amongst scholars what a 'Wittgensteinian conception' of philosophy is. For overviews of parts of the discussion, see, for instance, Bronzo (2012), Pleasants (2008), Crary (2000b) and Christensen (2003, 2011).

[3] To avoid some of the critiques, which have been directed at other thinkers who also have found it useful to direct their attention towards 'the ordinary' and 'the everyday' (see, e.g. Zigon 2014, 2019; Robbins 2016), I must underline that this advice only applies when we seek to understand a phenomenon familiar from our ordinary lives. If we seek to understand, for example, what 'measurement', 'particle' and 'experiment' amounts to in quantum physics, we should not consult our everyday understanding of these words but investigate and describe the uses of these words in this particular field of physics. Also, if we (as individuals, as participants in a practice, or as a society), for example, seek to understand a novel situation, where our old concepts find no—or no good—application, the philosophical task is also not only descriptive, but can also be critical, creative and inventive. I will return this theme several times in the following.

forms of life, as language is intertwined with and expresses forms of life: Our conventions, values, beliefs, practices, institutions and so forth (Wittgenstein 2009: § 23; Moi 2017: 41).

In this book I look at examples of moral change mainly in connection with the practice of law, a choice of focus explained in Part I. The point of doing so is to gain an understanding of the *dynamics* and *structures* of moral changes in Part I, and further to use the narratives of these changes as a vehicle for philosophically discussing the questions about the *normativity* of moral change in Part II. What I have done is to investigate how legal historians, legal practitioners, social scientists and legal documents describe and display moral changes, how these changes evolve and what dynamics have created them. In this manner I have let the practice of law both remind and teach me how moral changes unfold. Further, I have also used literature, the works of moral and legal philosophers as well as moral anthropologists to inform my thinking on the subject.

However, choosing and using legal historical research and other kind of 'case materials' in philosophy is never straightforward business—in more than one sense '*just* look and see' is not an option (see, e.g. Pitt 2001; Burian 2001; Widlok 2013; Bolinska and Martin 2019). One reason for this is that history does not deliver its cases to us in tiny Maggi-cubes, sharply cut out and ready-made for use. Historical cases have to be constructed (Eldridge 2016: 4–5, 28–30). In this construction, choices necessarily have to be made, for instance, as to "what happened; who was involved; which factors were most salient?" (Bolinska and Martin 2019: 3). A potential problem in this is that "bias can enter at every stage: the construction, selection, interpretation, and application of case studies create the possibility [...] that philosophical prejudices will shape them" (Bolinska and Martin 2019: 3, 6).[4] And not only philosophical prejudices but all other kinds of prejudices too. There are thus ways of using historical case materials in philosophy that are academically unwarranted, for instance, to cherry-pick cases that support one's theory, to ignore counterexamples and to rush into overgeneralisations.

In the choice and construction of cases of moral changes, I have relied on three main criteria. First, the cases given are chosen based on the

[4] Bolinska and Martin divide the challenges to the use of historical cases in philosophy into two categories—the aforementioned methodological challenges, and what they term 'metaphysical challenges'. I address the first here, and return (though indirectly) to the latter in Part II as part of dealing with what I term 'sceptical doubts'.

understanding of ethics as something to a large degree quotidian and familiar. Moral issues and moral uses of words are as well-known to us as any other everyday form of use (Wittgenstein 2009: § 77; 2006: 28). They are part of our ordinary practical rationality (Crary 2007b: 301). Normal, adult humans are thus, *ceteris paribus*, able to pick out examples of moral change. For Part I, I have attempted to pick ordinary examples of moral change, that is, cases which in everyday conversations are referred to or could be recognised as examples of moral change. Other philosophers such as Appiah (2010), Kitcher (2011), Buchanan and Powell (2016, 2018), Moody-Adams (2017), Pleasants (2018), Jaeggi (2018) and Baker (2019) have chosen similar cases in their work as examples of 'moral progress' or 'moral revolutions', both of which are forms of moral change. Thus, I have not attempted to avoid the cultural-moral biases, which lie in this criterion of choice (see Widlok 2013).[5] In the following, I do speak from a certain cultural and historical background—what is 'ordinary' and 'everyday' for me will not be so for every potential reader, neither in the present nor in the future. I am, however, not strongly wedded to the examples given. As mentioned, several of the cases chosen are examples of what are considered moral progress in much current moral philosophy. But these cases can be and are by others considered as examples of grave moral decline, like children's rights, church marriage for homosexuals and indigenous land rights.[6] What I hope is fairly uncontroversial across cultures and ideologies is that the cases chosen can be seen as examples of *moral change*, no matter what ethical evaluation the change merits. This, however, is also not guaranteed—what people consider a *moral* issue is one of the things that change over time and varies between people and peoples.

I further believe that other cases could have been chosen displaying both similar and different dynamics and structures than the ones I have chosen. For instance, one example encountered several times in my

[5] Blindly succumbing to cultural-moral biases entail the possibility of "misrepresentations of 'distant' forms of moral behaviour on the basis of specific norms and values of the observer (e.g. nationalism, liberalism or Eurocentrism) [...] and more fundamental biases, such as blindness towards 'morality in action', the exaggeration of the importance of codified morality or the overemphasis of moral justifications in discussions of morality" (Widlok 2013: 20).

[6] For example, Archard (2015), Ishay (2008), Hunt (2008) and Grahn-Farley (2013) refer to human rights conventions as moral progress, and this is a fairly common conception of this legal change. But there are dissenting voices to the idea of human rights as moral progress, see, for instance, Zigon (2013).

research, but not elaborated much on in Part I, is 'the fire soul', so often the hero of movies and biographies—the person those strong ideological determination and struggle manages to create a moral change, or the 'first mover', who "defy convention and spearhead new behaviours", but not necessarily does so out of strong moral or ideological convictions (Bicchieri 2017: xv). Other untreated dynamics are, for example, how technological and medical innovations play into the creation of moral change. An example of the first could be the Danish politicians' decision to push the agenda of 'digital government' made possible by the recent developments in computer technology. One result of this is the ongoing transmission from manual and paper-based public administration to digital government (Motzfeldt and Næsborg-Andersen: 2018). Some legal scholars argue that this threatens to erode, and thus change, some of the basic moral values that hereto have been underlying and guiding the administration of the public sector. The birth control pill's influence on sexual morality is often seen as an example of the latter, being an important factor in 'de-moralising' sex before marriage in the Western parts of the world (Van der Burg 2003; Baker 2019: 115–152). This investigation is thus not covering everything we can learn about the dynamics and structures of moral change from history, anthropology, sociology, biology, economy, literature and others—and it does also not aim to do so, for reasons that will hopefully be clear at the end of the book, when I sketch the conception of 'the ethical' I term contextual ethics.

The second criterion for the choice of cases is to cover cases ranging from minor over medium to major and radical moral change. When investigating moral changes it is natural to become fascinated and focussed on examples of dramatic civil disobedience or moral revolutions, like Gandhi's rebellion, the French Revolution or the abolition of slavery, where whole societies changed some of their fundamental moral values and legal and political systems (see, e.g. Baker 2019; Pleasants 2018; Appiah 2010; Lear 2008; Berman 1983). In these cases, the moral changes are obvious and stand out, and the description of them furthermore often amounts to an engaging and thought provoking story. Yet, to understand the dynamics of moral change and moral normativity only from the point of view of revolutions and radical changes would, I believe, be problematic, as they do not amount to the most common kind of moral changes. Where cultural devastation and moral revolutions are fairly rare, minor moral changes, on the other hand, are not. Moral changes on a small scale are a constant aspect of human lives, and they unfold both on the level of the individual's life, in practices, and in whole societies. I have therefore also chosen cases, which are not 'moral revolutions', but still can be argued to be moral changes on a smaller scale. However, research on change in other areas, like Kuhn's work on changes in science (Kuhn 1970) as well as in moral philosophy, like Lear's work on cultural devastation (Lear 2008) and Baker's on moral revolutions (Baker 2019), show that issues of normativity—and thus activities such as evaluation, critique, justification and judging—take on different forms and roles in different degrees of change, most notably during and after radical changes. In order to discuss the normativity of moral changes, I have deemed it important to cover the 'full range' from minor to radical changes.

When categorising a particular change according to how wide-ranging it is, the categorisation depends on what one compares the change to and the perspective from where one looks at the change (from the perspective of the ant, which I step on and crush, this event is a major change in its world, for me this change is so tiny that I would say nothing really changed). It will therefore always be highly debatable how any concrete change, moral or otherwise, should be categorised in terms of 'size' and 'range'. When it comes to the cases discussed, I do not wish to make any factual claims about their size and range. What I do hope to have accomplished is to present meaningful descriptions of what minor and radical moral changes can look like.

Thirdly, and lastly, the main part of the examples is drawn from the practice of law in a broad sense of the term. This I have done as a too narrow focus more likely leads to a distorted conception of the phenomena one seeks to understand (Wittgenstein 2009; Widlok 2013; Bolinska and Martin 2019). The legal case material I have investigated therefore encompasses legal research comparing changes in morally important concepts in laws, international declarations and conventions, an ancient play on a moral conflict arising out of a change of law, legal and legislative history documenting what lead up to the passing of ethically significant new laws, national laws, social scientific investigations of changes in a people's moral values after the passing of new laws, and a lawyer's speaking notes for explaining cases, laws and court decisions to her clients and at seminars at universities.[7] On the basis of these materials I have constructed eight narratives of moral changes in Part I.

[7] Obviously, the objection could be raised that to truly avoid a too one-sided diet in my investigation, I also ought to have investigated, for instance, sociological, psychological,

What is done with legal historical research, laws and other 'case materials' in this book is inspired by Lear's philosophical use of anthropological and historical material in the work *Radical Hope*. Lear writes: "A philosophical inquiry may rely on historical and anthropological accounts of how a traditional culture actually came to an end, but ultimately it wants to know not about actuality but about possibility" (Lear 2008: 7–9). The eight narratives of moral changes have very different historical depths and precision. Some are more or less just mentioned and rely on not very authoritative sources, some are roughly sketched, and still others are described within the context of a longer historical background and based on the work of several authoritative historians. None of the narratives are constructed in a way that aims to satisfy the criteria and methods of, for example, history, sociology or legal dogmatics. For instance, no critical source analysis is made. Furthermore, if the historical literature I have read is silent or imprecise as to when and where a change happened, so is my narrative.

The main reason for these choices is that the investigation in this book is philosophical and hence has other aims, methods and criteria of success than, for example, historical, sociological and legal research (Wittgenstein 2009: §§ 89–133, xii; Kuusela 2008; Hacker 2015). The aim is not to supply the reader with new, accurate and reliable historical information—but to supply us with a clear conceptual understanding of moral change and to address moral worries and sceptical doubts. The nature of the cases below is best understood if they are viewed as narratives of various moral changes inspired by and based on legal, historical, and sociological research as well as on legal texts like conventions, speaking notes and laws. The stories are vehicles for philosophical thinking by being descriptions of moral changes. The relevant questions to ask of these narratives are thus generally not 'Is this true? Did things really happen this way at this point in time? Was the dynamic x actually why y changed?' (even though it is in some cases). Rather, the questions to ask are 'Does this narrative *make sense* as a story about a conflict which leads to moral change?' or 'Is this story enlightening as to what *could* be a dynamic leading to moral change?'

neurological, biological and economic, research into various forms of moral changes. Further, my theoretical fame could have been wider or different and so forth. With a topic as broad as 'moral change' the possibilities of meaningful critique of my choice of focus as well as theoretical frame are countless. What I present is not the only good or an exhaustive way of investigating this topic, but hopefully one fruitful way of doing so.

The central concept in this work is that of 'moral change'. The last reason for investigating moral change, I want to bring forth here, is that despite there since the 1980s has been an increasing interest in and awareness of the historicity of morality, then moral change as such is currently under-theorised (Hämäläinen 2017: 47–48). The main focus in contemporary philosophy is on 'moral progress' (see, e.g. Nussbaum 2007, 2011; Rorty 1999, 2007; Posner 1998a, b; Moody-Adams 1999, 2002, 2017; Singer 2008; Wilson 2010; Appiah 2010; Pleasants 2010, 2018; Roth 2012; Summers 2016; Jamieson 2016; Musschenga and Meynen 2017; Buchanan and Powell 2016, 2018; Hermann 2019). The topic of moral change as such, the dynamics creating it and the structures it unfolds after thus represents a lacuna in the existing moral philosophical research.

The concept of 'moral change' will, for reasons also made clear in the concluding section on contextual ethics, remain a fairly broad term throughout this book. If one consults a dictionary, 'change' means "make or become different".[8] Change is further characterised by being a timely phenomenon—it unfolds between a before and an after. But when, and thus also why, something begins to change is in many cases difficult to pinpoint exactly and will often be debatable. As a novice to reading historical research, I often found myself being drawn further and further back in time in my search for an understanding of the dynamics leading to any event in the present. Trying to understand the passing of the *Convention of the Rights of the Child* in the UN in 1989 thus lead me back to laws and legal conceptions of the child in the early Roman Empire (Vial-Dumas 2014)! When creating a historical narrative there is often an element of arbitrary choice in the starting point. The narratives in Part I are no exception to this rule.

What, then, 'becomes different' in a *moral* change? That is up for heated philosophical debate; a debated entered in Part II. In this book, 'moral change' refers to, for instance, a law going from giving an incitement to cause human harm to not doing so. A moral change can also be a change in how we believe we best take care of something we value (like good health), where the value stays the same, but we gain new knowledge of the world, which changes how well we manage to live up to this value. A moral change can also be a change in what we morally value or condemn in our society, like the change from valuing 'obedience' in the education of children to putting more stress on 'an ability to critical thinking'. A

[8] https://en.oxforddictionaries.com/definition/change (accessed 12.4.2019).

moral change can further be a change in our moral framework and ideals, like when 'honour' was abandoned as a core ideal for family life in Scandinavia. Such row of examples seems, however, to leave it an open question precisely what it is that changes in what we refer to as 'a moral change'. Is it ever morality itself that changes? Or is it only human understanding of morality, or the circumstances, which morality is applied to, which changes? (Raz 1994: 144; Green 2013a: 480; Moody-Adams 2017: 2–3). An important task for contemporary research, and one which is dealt with throughout this book, is thus to discuss which metaphors and conceptualisations are apt for understanding morality. With this book my hope has been that attention to moral changes in the contexts of actual life combined with philosophical discussions proves a fruitful road to travel towards an understanding of the both elusive and tangible phenomenon of moral change.

PART I

# The Dynamics and Structures of Moral Change

> Modern moralities differ enormously from tribal worlds of Leviticus and Deuteronomy or the heroic societies of the Odyssey and Beowulf. We have gone from thinking that an insult to familial honour is adequate justification for killing another, to thinking that would be plain murder; from thinking slavery is permissible and even natural to holding it a grotesque assault on human dignity. These are not merely changes in the social facts on which morality operates, they are changes in social morality itself. (Green 2013a: 480)

What drives moral changes like the legal prohibition of slavery and women's right to vote? The importance of an answer to this question lies in its role in active creations of social and moral change in societies. For instance, both Bicchieri and Appiah rely on that general knowledge or a theory of the dynamics of change can help us to create changes in harmful practices, institutions and traditions, like honour killing, child marriage, genital mutilation and political corruption (Bicchieri 2017: ix–xi; Appiah 2010: xvii, 139–172). Further, a wrong or insufficient conceptualization, held by, for example, scientists, politicians and NGOs and incorporated into laws and institutions, can lead to misfired inventions, wasted resources and possibly human harm. If we lack conceptual clarity, we will have trouble making good decisions (Hopf 2018: 688). In other words, the value of an adequate understanding of the dynamics and structures of moral changes lies in its potential to help or hinder us create progress.

The research into the topic of moral change has several lacunas, one of which is that "We lack a general account of the springs of moral change" (Green 2013a: 481)—we lack a general understanding of what leads to and creates moral changes. There has been both empirical and philosophical research into the dynamics and structure of moral revolutions (e.g. Palmer and Schagrin 1978; Appiah 2010; Pleasants 2018; Hermann 2019; Baker 2019), into how certain individuals or a certain people have changed their moral outlook (e.g. Robbins 2004, 2007; Lear 2008; Minnameier 2009; Roth 2012), into which metaphors we use to understand moral changes (e.g. Hämäläinen 2017), and into how social norms, affecting important moral issues, change and can be changed (e.g. Bicchieri 2017; Sunstein 2019). However, we still lack an understanding of the dynamics and structures of moral changes as such, ranging from minor to revolutionary changes. In the following, I will unfold why I consider practices of law to be a particular suited focus for a philosophical investigation into moral change.[1]

The discussion of the nature of the relations between law and ethics has ancient roots, and has not been settled to this day.[2] It therefore seems prudent to follow Green and Hart in the conclusions that "The single most important thing to know about the relationship between law and morality is that there is no single thing to know" (Green 2013b: 1). This is because "There are many different types of relation between law and morals and there is nothing which can be profitably singled out for study as *the* relation between them" (Hart 1997: 185, my italics). The work in this book thus rests on the assumption that law and ethics are connected in various ways. "Law is a normative social practice" (Delacroix 2011: 155), and part of that normativity is of an ethical nature (Delacroix 2011: 147,148; Van Der Burg 2014: 71). Laws and legal institutions institutionalise moral values and ideals of the society we want to keep, as well as visions of the society we do not yet have but seek to create (Green 2013a: 494).

Although law can incarnate parts of a society's moral ideas and ideals, the two concepts are not synonyms: Everything 'legal' is not 'ethical', and vice versa. This leads to what can be called law's inherent moral risk (Delacroix 2017). There can be a difference in what the law demands of us and what morality demands of us, for example, in the form of love,

[1] In legal science there is no general agreement on the definition of law (see e.g. Gardner 2011; Del Mar 2011: 1; Marmor 2015; Patterson 2010). I follow Patterson (1990: 980), Morawetz (2000a) and Eisele (2006) in conceptualizing law as *a practice* (or, more precisely, a set of practices, as law is and has been practiced in different ways).

[2] Moore (2012) gives an insight into how complex the question and current debates of the relations between law and morality are in legal philosophy today.

justice or respect of family—something Sophocles' ancient play *Antigone* reminds us: Antigone, daughter of Oedipus, is caught in a grim dilemma. Her brother, Polyneices, has been killed in a battle over the throne of Thebes. Religion and tradition demand that dead relatives should be buried by the family, and she feels morally obliged to follow this. Yet the King, Antigone's uncle Creon, has decreed that Polyneices' corpse should be left on the open plain to rot. Antigone chooses to obey the moral law, break the King's law and bury her brother. Afterwards she has to face the angry king and explain her disobedience, which she does with an eloquent skill for insult and youth's undying contempt of power and death:

> Creon: [...] did you know of the proclamation forbidding this?
>
> Antigone: I knew. How could I not? It was public knowledge.
>
> Creon: And yet you dared to break this law?
>
> Antigone: Yes; for it was not Zeus who made this proclamation to me; not did Justice who dwells with the gods below lay down these laws for mankind. Nor did I think that your human proclamation had sufficient power to override the unwritten, unassailable laws of the gods. They live not just yesterday and today, but forever, and no-one knows when they first came to light. I was not going to incur punishment from the gods, not in fear of the will of any man. I knew I must die—how could I not?—even if you had not made your proclamation. But if I am to die before my time, then I call that a gain; for someone who lives in the midst of evils as I do, how could it not be an advantage to die? So for me to meet this fate is no pain at all. But if I had allowed the dead son of my mother to remain unburied, then I would have suffered; as it is, I feel no pain. If I now seem to you to have acted foolishly, perhaps I am convicted of folly by a fool. (Sophocles 2003: 33–35)

Creon probably did not make this particular law with the intention of doing good, but in order to get even. Yet even if he had tried to do good, this would not have been a guarantee of success. The open, transcending nature of the ethical excludes an exhaustive codification of it, so the demands of law and ethics will always run the risk of running up against each other.

Another important difference between the normativity of law and that of ethics is that we do not get to choose what morality demands of us. That it is bad to cause suffering is not so because we have agreed upon it or decided it to be so. But in principle, though not always in practice for the single individual or group, "Law is different. We do get to choose what our law requires of us. […] Law is always subject to deliberate choice" (Green 2013a: 475). We as a society—or our representatives or our tyrants—get to choose what is demanded of us legally.

Moral changes can, as mentioned in the introduction, among other things be changes in what is valued and strived for, in how we conceive our duties, obligations and commitments, in what we are prepared to label as wrong and harmdoing and and how we deal with wrong and harmdoing. A lot of this is reflected in the legal practice of a society because law is one of the ways in which societies deal with the shifting demands of what life ethically asks of us. Law and laws can thus be seen as both ethically *insufficient* and ethically *indispensable* (Fink 2007: 55). When humans make law, they mean business—they do not in general stipulate law about matters considered unimportant or petty, and among these important concerns are ethical concerns. We are willing to punish ethical wrongdoings and omissions in more severe ways than when someone breaks the rules of good table manners or lacks aesthetic sensitivity (Hanfling 2003: 27). Significant changes in a society's morality will for that reason often be reflected in changes of law (Hart 1997: 185; Green 2013a: 479). Much can therefore be learned about moral change through the history of changes in laws, legal practices and institutions. Moreover, the changes in law can often be traced because many societies *document* law. The oldest known written source of law is carved in stone, namely the *Code of Hammurabi*, which is approximately 4000 years old (Andersen 2011b: 71). Humans declare laws publicly, they carve laws onto stone, write them down in books, explain the purpose of them in preambles, make the results of law cases public on official webpages, report about them in newspapers, announce the laws publicly and write legal and legislative history and all of this are sources available for a philosopher.

In this part of the book, a philosophical investigation of the structures and dynamics of moral change is conducted through eight narratives mainly inspired by the practice of law. The eight stories are "recollections marshalled for a particular purpose" (Wittgenstein 2009: § 127), in this case the purpose of eliciting an overview and understanding of how and why morality can change.

CHAPTER 2

# Angel Makers and the Swedish Child Care Laws of 1902

> Hilda pauses a few minutes outside the door, listening for sounds in the room behind her. She knows there cannot be any sound to hear, yet she always lingers and listens, nonetheless. This is the hardest part. The time where it still can be undone, where she can stop it from happening, the deed, the drowning. This time the unwanted had been a boy. He was more nourished and bigger than the other infants had been. She freezes. Perhaps. Perhaps he does have the strengths to lift the lid even though she had weighed it down with the coal scuttle? Hilda holds her breath. No. Not a sound. She walks off to take care of the laundry.

By the end of the nineteenth century, the conception of children and how to treat them was undergoing a significant change in the legal systems of Europe and other parts of the Western world. As a tiny part of this larger movement, the Swedish government in 1902 passed laws with the aim of better protection of criminal, neglected and orphaned children; the bad conditions of which they had become aware (Grahn-Farley 2013: 151–153). Before 1902, the situation in Sweden was indeed grim:

> The social regimes in place during this period with respect to children living outside the protection of the family unit were few and brutal. An *Änglamakerska* (Angel maker) was a woman who was effectively paid to treat a child so badly and neglectfully that it died. Another form of social practice for dealing with such children was *Sockengång*, which meant that a child without means had to move between different private households, which took turns in providing for the child. (Grahn-Farley 2013: 150–151)


C. Eriksen, *Moral Change*,
https://doi.org/10.1007/978-3-030-61037-1_2

According to the 1871 statute *Fattigvårdsförördningen* (poverty care ordinance), the government could provide 'poverty housing' or placement in private homes for the orphan, where the child had to work in return for housing and food (Grahn-Farley 2013: 152). Placement of unsupported children would occur after the child had been auctioned off to the lowest bidder—that is, the family that requested the least compensation from the state for taking the child in (Grahn-Farley 2013: 153). This resulted in conditions where many of the children practically lived like slaves, and in the worst cases were killed. In the latter cases, the foster parents either intentionally made the children "live in penury and starvation to the point where they finally died." (Högman 2017) or, more rarely, killed the child by strangling or drowning.

The practice of mistreating or killing the children in order to collect the state money for taking care of them was so common not only in Sweden, but throughout the West that there were names for it. It was referred to as 'angel-making' and 'baby-farming'. Baby-farming was an occupational practice known in the UK, the USA, New Zealand, Australia, Denmark and Sweden (*Encyclopædia Britannica*: 97). "Unwanted children everywhere throughout the West [from ancient times to modern age] were often disposable, killed as infants or abandoned to institutions or to the streets. The history of infanticide [...] is long and winding [...]" (Fass 2013: 4; see also Dübeck 2013: 75–77). In 1871 in the UK, the House of Commons had appointed a committee to investigate the conditions in baby-farms in order "to inquire as to the best means of preventing the destruction of the lives of infants". They noted: "Improper and insufficient food [...] opiates, drugs, crowded rooms, bad air, want of cleanliness, and wilful neglect are sure to be followed in a few months by diarrhoea, convulsions and wasting away" (*Encyclopædia Britannica*: 97).

Even so, at this point of time in the West it was not legal to severely neglect or kill foster-children. The criminal laws did to some extent—at least in theory—protect children from grave harm. For instance in the UK around 1700–1800, children were protected "against severely injurious or life-threatening acts perpetrated against them by their parents" (Eekelaar 1986: 167). A child, on the other hand, who hit her or his parent, would often face severe legal punishment—under a Swedish law of 1734, this punishment could go up to death penalty. The moral values informing these laws were that good Christian children should honour and obey their parents. Good Christian parents, on the other hand, had no reciprocal obligation to honour their child, as Grahn-Farley dryly points out

(Grahn-Farley 2013: 151). Despite the formal legal protection of children's lives through the criminal law, some angel-makers went undetected for years. In their legislative work on children in 1902, the Swedish government particularly wanted to stop the practice of angel-makers (Grahn-Farley 2013: 153–4).

> Unfortunately, the law had the opposite effect and further encouraged the dreadful practice. Under the 1902 foster care law, the foster home received a lump sum intended to last until the child reached adulthood. This meant the profit to the foster home per child was higher the earlier the child died, which encouraged the angel-makers. (Grahn-Farley 2013: 154)

The most infamous known case of angel-making in Sweden was Hilda Nilsson, who operated years after the passing of the child care laws. Between 1915 and 1917 Nilsson drowned eight of her foster children (Grahn-Farley 2013: 154). She would place the infants in a small tub filled with water, put a lid and a heavy coal scuttle on top, leave the room for some hours and return to find the infant dead. She would then burn or bury the body. Only two of her foster children were allowed to live. Hilda Nilsson was caught, when a mother wanted to see her son, Gunnar, and Nilsson would not allow her. The mother became suspicious and alarmed the foster care board (*Fosterbarnsnämnden*), who involved the police, and the case then unravelled (Högman 2017).

It was not only in Sweden that governments around 1900 had begun taking action in order to protect the lives of orphaned and poor children. Similar acts and laws were enacted in other places in Europe in order to turn baby-farming into a practice less harmful for the children: In the UK 'The Infant Life Protection Act 1897' and the 'Children Act 1908' were passed. In South Australia the 'State Children Act of 1895' and in New Zealand the 'Adoption of Children Act 1895' and the 'Infant Life Protection Act 1896' were passed (*Encyclopædia Britannica*: 97). In Sweden, after critique in the early 1930s of how the Swedish government failed to take good care of orphaned children, who at that point still lived under harsh and punitive conditions, the child care laws of 1902 were subsequently changed again (Grahn-Farley 2013: 164). This time with a somewhat better outcome.

One of the things this piece of legal history on the 1902 child care laws in Sweden can remind us of, is that humans often choose to change their practices, when they discover a practice is resting on a mistake and because of that misses its objective. The Swedish politicians aimed to relieve the sufferings of children with the 1902 laws, but failed to do so due to their flawed legal construction, and instead the laws led to increased suffering and abuse. This moral decline happened, because the laws gave a strong economic incentive to take up the practice of angel-making. When the politicians finally faced up to the mistake in the construction of the law, it was, eventually, changed, and changed for the better.

CHAPTER 3

# Turning the Other Cheek with a Check in the Hand

It is early spring at a kindergarten playground in Uppsala. The air is thin and cold. Birds fill the sky with joyful courtship, and tiny flowers parade delicate colours against the damp brown and grey of the fallen winter. In the sandpit, a couple of three-year olds move around in their snowsuits, miniature astronauts exploring the world still new to them. At one point they start to interact. Something is being built. Suddenly, screaming rips up the serenity. There is a fight. Mighty anger is displayed over the ownership of the yellow shovel. A pedagogue comes over, sits down and calmly asks one of the children: 'So, what's going on here? Why did you hit her?' The answer is given pronto, in a voice quivering with indignation, '*She hit me first!*'.

This is a common scene and conversation between adults and kindergarten children, and it expresses what seems to be a basic human instinct and sense of justice. If someone hurts you, you are likely to want payback and will, depending on your age and upbringing, feel justified in doing so. "When people wrong you, says conventional wisdom, you should use justified rage to put them in their place, exact a penalty" (Nussbaum 2016: 1). This sense of justice is called the law of retaliation. Institutionalised, written down versions of it can be found, for instance, in the Bible, the Koran (Sharia Law) and the Code of Hammurabi (Andersen 2011b: 71; Anners 1998: 28–30).

For millennia, in large parts of the world, 'an eye for an eye and a tooth for a tooth' was a predominant code in societies for dealing with situations, when someone was hurt by someone else. The principle was not,


C. Eriksen, *Moral Change*,
https://doi.org/10.1007/978-3-030-61037-1_3

however, as it is natural to conceive it today, a rule about the relation between individuals, because in this period the individual was rarely a subject of law. It was a code for the relation between families (kin) (Anners 1998: 13–16). If one of your kin was damaged or killed, you had the legal right and a strong moral duty to retaliate and take revenge by damaging a member of the perpetrator's kin (Fenger 1971: 65). And so people did, earning names for themselves such as Thorfinn Skull-splitter.

From time to time, this practice would evolve into regular feuds between different families, leaving a trail, typically of dead young men, behind, as vividly described in the Islandic Sagas, which, if published today, would have been titled *50 Shades of Bloody Red*:

> In time Eirik's thralls caused a landslide to crash down upon the farm of Valthjof at Valthjofsstadir, where upon Valthjof's kinsman Eyjolf Saur killed the thralls by Skeidsbrekka above Vatnshorn. For this Eirik killed Eyolf Saur. He killed Holmgang-Hrafn too at Leikskalar. Gerstein and Odd of Jorvi, both kinsmen of Eyolf's, took up his case, and Eirik was driven out of Haukadal. (Jones 2008: 127–128)

This understanding of justice and moral duty to kin led to never-ending spirals of violent vengeance, which sometimes destroyed whole families and devastated villages, and this in times when strong arms and backs were needed in order to bring food to the table, and where war, starvation and diseases already claimed the lion's share of the population. The law of retaliation, when put into practice on this level and in this manner, was thus deeply harming to the possibility of not only human flourishing, but also of sheer human survival—in spite of the fact that the code seems to express a sense of justice natural to humans. Therefore, a change was called for.

Moral and religious arguments against the also morally, religiously, and legally sanctioned law of retaliation and the practice of vengeance were known long before it ceased to exist in European and Scandinavian legal systems and as a cultural practice. Most famous among these are probably the teachings in the New Testament. Here we meet the new radical idea of 'turning the other cheek', when someone hurts you. But clearly, neither the emergence of this idea nor a very politically and culturally influential and widespread religion preaching it did on its own manage to end the practice of violent vengeance—that is, the mere knowledge of this unnatural option of action did not do the transformative trick. Only turning the other cheek was not recognised as a meaningful solution to the problem of feuds.

The solution came by adding two other ingredients to the mix: The first extra ingredient was interpreting the principle of equality implicit in the practice in a more abstract manner (Anners 1998: 16). In some societies, 'an eye for an eye' was taken to be a principle that required a literal interpretation (Andersen 2011b: 71). Did you by accident or intentionally cut off someone's right hand, the just punishment was that your right hand had to be cut off too. In other societies, it had been acceptable to inflict a *similar*, and not necessarily identical, bodily damage on the other part (Andersen 2011b: 71). But the new way of understanding the principle of equality in relation to feuds was altogether to abandon retaliation in terms of physical harm and instead introduce the idea of paid damages. A family could be paid equivalent damages in the form of money, sheep or other goods, when a family member was damaged or killed by another family. "This is why the oldest existing records of legal rules in kin-based societies first of all are catalogues of the size of the compensation which the offending kin has to pay if it wants to achieve reconciliation" (Anners 1998: 16, my translation).

The other ingredient of the solution to the problem was allowing a neutral third party to intervene and play a role in this kind of conflicts between families. Up until this point in history, the family in many ways was a legally sealed sphere, but now harm was no longer considered a private matter between families. It became a matter for the society. The neutral third party could be a chief, a king, a people's council, or a state official, depending on the time in history and the form of society (Anners 1998: 13, 17). This third party could act as a legislator, setting up the compensation system, as a mediator, judge, and law enforcer in case one of the families was not complying with what had been decided. Thus, involving a powerful, neutral third party in the feud and getting 'a damages check', was what finally made the turn of the cheek obviously not easy, but doable in enough instances as to end the feuds and the practice of physical vengeance as the normal way of reacting to harm in Scandinavia—except in kindergartens.

In the first instance, this moral change (the change from having a practice undermining the flourishing of societies, families and individuals to having one which to a higher degree was protecting the possibility of flourishing) was initiated by the fact that the old practice of vengeance had led to the killing and molesting of too many human beings, which caused not only suffering and grief but also made some families and small societies face extinction. What made the transformation of the practice possible was inspiration from a radically different ethical idea (turn the other cheek) combined with the pragmatic legal idea of paid damages and an effective institutional setting (i.e. a third, neutral power instance setting up the compensation rules, judging the damages, capable of holding families accountable for paying the decided damages, and taking over the punishment of them, if they did not comply). The 'turning of cheek' in this story is thus not the Christian turn of a cheek, which entails to give up the logic of retaliation altogether.

This narrative reminds us that a practice creating sufferings and threatening to extinguish us is a strong motivational reason for us to change it. But the story also points to a basic fact of human existence: A solution which works with and not against any natural inclinations is important in creating a successful ethical change. The compensation system makes use of what seems to be a natural sense of justice, because the other part in the conflict still suffers financially in return for the suffering they create. The spread of this new legal practice for dealing with harm that humans inflict on each other was a change with great moral implications, but it is not a radical moral change in the sense of the new practice being incommensurable with the old one, because having to pay damages still means that a kind of harm is inflicted on the perpetrator in retaliation for her harmdoing—the perpetrator still has to pay for what she did.

CHAPTER 4

# The Obedient Danes and the Smoking Law

The biggest book fair of the year is approaching. At the aspiring University Press in Aarhus editors work round the clock, each herding their own unruly band of authors, reviewers, proofreaders, graphic artists and printing houses forward, making sure no one strays from the agreed upon path of deadlines. During the weekly editorial meeting, attendants are fiddling with their lukewarm coffee mugs, many are smoking, and all, one by one, give reports to the director on how manuscripts fare in the production process. As the meeting progresses, the room slowly fills with blue smoke, forming thick layers and lazily drifting in spirals towards the sealing.

Before 2007, it was legal to smoke almost everywhere in Denmark. Danes knew smoking was harmful to themselves and those in their proximity (MM/TF 2017: 48), but nonetheless the practice of smoking was deeply engraved and valued in Danish culture (Andersen 2011a: 8–9, 73)—so much so that in 2000 the Minister of Health, Carsten Koch, was overthrown because he suggested a law regulating smoking in public places! (MM/TF 2008: 16). For more than a hundred years it had been completely normal and morally accepted for people to smoke in bars, restaurants, workplaces and public transportation. It was as natural as drinking a cup of coffee. Also teachers, pedagogues, parents and grandparents smoked in the company of children in homes, schools, and even in childcare (Ibid.: 20; MM/TF 2017: 61). The Danish people would, according to sociologist Jørgen Goul Andersen, even have considered it to some


C. Eriksen, *Moral Change*,
https://doi.org/10.1007/978-3-030-61037-1_4

extent 'un-Danish' not to smoke almost anywhere and anytime anyone felt like it. It was, for instance, considered rude and health-zealous, if a host asked a smoker not to smoke during dinner in the former person's own home. Today, however, as people in the most of Europe and Northern America, Danes do not smoke in any of these places, and also often not even in their own homes (Ibid.: 48–53). What brought this change around?

On 29 May 2007 the law, which is commonly known as 'The Smoking Law' (Lov om røgfri miljøer), was passed by all parties in the Danish Parliament, except by one party, who abstained from voting, but only because they did not find the law restrictive enough.[1] The declared aim of the law is "to spread smoke-free environments in order to prevent harmful effects of passive smoking and prevent anyone from involuntarily being subjected to passive smoking" (Act No. 512 of 6 June 2007, Chapter 1, Section 1, my translation). This aim was sought realised by forbidding smoking in all public buildings, workplaces, schools, institutions, collective transportation and 'serving places' (ibid., Chapter 1, Section 2). The law also includes a ban on smoking in private homes, while public servants are working there, for instance, during elder care (ibid., Chapter 3, Section 12).

The reason for making the law was an increasing knowledge of the damaging effects on human health of not only active, but also passive smoking. Passive smoking was deemed responsible for the death of 2000 people every year in Denmark, which is far more than are killed in total in traffic and by murder. Passive smoking had also been proven to be responsible for sufferings like cancer, heart diseases, asthma, bronchitis, SIDS and other diseases, which not least affect children (Astma-Allergi Forbundet, et al. 2005).[2] The politicians' focus on the harmful effects of active and passive smoking was part of a larger national as well as international 'health trend', and the Danish State tried to secure and control the health of its citizens not only through laws directly restricting smoking, but also by putting appalling pictures and guilt provoking messages on cigarette packets, by placing extra taxes on sugar and fat, and by informing citizens of the so-called extra public expenses to health care for smoking, excessively overweight, and alcohol drinking citizens.

[1] Lov nr. 512 of 06/06/2007 (https://www.retsinformation.dk/forms/r0710.aspx?id=11388), which was later modified by Lov nr. 607 of 18/06/2012 (https://www.retsinformation.dk/Forms/R0710.aspx?id=142456).

[2] https://www.retsinformation.dk/eli/ft/200614L00535.

When the Smoking Law was passed, it was met with massive critique by many Danes and especially by owners of clubs, cafés and restaurants (MM/TF 2017: 48). A group of the latter even took the Danish State to court to fight for the right of guests to smoke in their establishments, and for a while, some ordinary citizens took to civil disobedience and broke the law by still smoking in restaurants, workplaces and schools. However, within less than six months, the vast majority of Danes did not only obey the law, but they had also changed their views on smoking as well as their smoking practice. Today, Danes value smoke-free environments far higher than their freedom to smoke (MM/TF 2008: 5, 27, 46; 2017: 9). A smoker is now also considered a slightly morally bad person—someone with a lack of spine, who pollutes the air and other people's health, and who is responsible for being a burden to the welfare society. Smoking is thus not morally neutral any longer, like coffee drinking still is. The moral changes displayed here are a shift from the smokers not protecting the health of others to actually doing so, as well as a people going from valuing personal freedom and enjoyment highest, to valuing the care of other people's health higher; changes, which some Danes consider 'a cultural revolution' (Lose 2018). What explains this rapid moral transformation?

The Smoking Law was passed, as earlier mentioned, because the politicians found the increasing scientific knowledge and evidences of a causal connection between not only active but also passive smoking and damaging consequences to peoples' health convincing. Here the dynamic behind the legal change was that those in power took scientific knowledge seriously (and, a cynic might add, they created an opportunity to tax tobacco even further and save expenses in health care). Yet, knowledge of a damage-causing causal chain cannot have been the main dynamics behind the fast change in the moral values and smoking practice of the Danish population. This is so because this knowledge had been around for decades and had not in itself stopped the Danes from smoking. However, this general knowledge in the population was most likely part of the context, which enabled the rapid transformation to unfold, though it was not the triggering factor.

A tricking factor for the change was the passing of the Smoking Law (MM/TF 2008: 20; Malacinski 2011), but to explain the pace and thoroughness of the change, we also have to look at another dynamic, as the world has seen plenty of laws being passed without eliciting any changes. The other main explanatory factor still needed in this case is the fact that

Danes are a very law-abiding people. Andersen has documented that Danes generally obey the law, *because* it is the law (Andersen 2011a: 8, 57–60).

> In concluding, it can be said that Danes' ability to comply with regulations is quite remarkable. On the one hand, Danes have quite strong traditions for opposition to too much central control, and there is probably also a limit somewhere, where a regulation that is contrary to their norms can be lost on them, and maybe even destroy their respect for the laws. However, this limit is far off. The typical reaction is exactly the opposite: Danes will soon come to respect new rules and assimilate them as part of the general norm: the law of the land must (by and large) be respected. (Andersen 2011a: 60, my translation)

Danes' practice of smoking and the moral evaluation of the practice and its participants could thus change so rapidly, because the Danes do what the law asks of them, and not, as it is tempting to assume, because the majority of Danes' moral values and view on smoking had changed first. In the 'smoking law case' we thus witness law-created moral changes. Not only do Danes now morally value and thus seek to create 'smoke-free environments', but they also morally condemn smoking and to some extent smokers. Furthermore, the particular human vulnerability, which the politicians intended to protect by the Smoking Law, is in fact better protected after the passing of the law than before, because the Danes obey the law. People, who were previously unwilling passive smokers in places where they often could not avoid being—like babies in day-care, children in kindergartens and in schools, people in workplaces and elderly people in nursing homes—are no longer exposed to smoke, and their health is better protected due to that. The scientific discovery of links between a certain practice and damages to human health, the spread of this knowledge, the passing of laws combined with a very law-abiding people were the dynamics leading to these moral changes in a practice and a people's moral outlook.

CHAPTER 5

# A Rebirth of Justice? Indigenous Land Rights in Canada

> She had never appreciated the expression 'the calm before the storm'. Where she lived, there was hard wind, when a storm was approaching, making the rusty roofs on the tool sheds rattle and the lake sing in low growling voices between the rocks on the shore. Today, however, before the trial is set to begin, there is a moment of utter silence in the courtroom. She let herself be filled with its dignified calm, praying it will last through the storm of falsehoods she and her people are about to face, praying that her voice will be heard through it.

In the area now known as Canada, humans have been living for thousands of years. These peoples, today referred to as Indigenous Peoples, were living mainly as hunters, gatherers, fishers and farmers. Some of the 1.8 million Indigenous Peoples living in Canada today can trace back their history in the area more than 3000 years, like the *Haida* and the *Gitxsan*. They first interacted with European hunters and traders around 1000 AD, but sustained contact was not established until the Europeans settled in the seventeenth and eighteenth centuries.[1] For the Indigenous Peoples this contact proved fatal in many cases, and in all cases harmful to their way of life.

Yet, in Canada, unlike many other parts of the world getting in touch with the European colonisers, the land was not conquered (Mandell

[1] http://www.thecanadianencyclopedia.ca/en/article/aboriginal-people/. Accessed 15.7.2017.



C. Eriksen, *Moral Change*,
https://doi.org/10.1007/978-3-030-61037-1_5

2015a: 1; Harhoff 1993: 366). The traders, and later settlers, were welcomed, and over time different numbered treaties on the use of land were negotiated between the indigenous population and the reigning monarch of Canada: 'the Crown' in the UK (Mandell and Pinder 2012: 2; Harhoff 1993: 377). This was done according to the Royal Proclamation of 1763, stating that if aboriginal title has *not* been dealt with, then the land and its resources are not available "as a source of revenue" (Mandell 2015b: 2; see also Harhoff 1993: 372). This means that throughout Canada's history and through Canada's constitution, there is "a bedrock of legal pluralism. [...] This law and the Treaties endowed Canada with an Indigenous foundation based on the rule of law" (Mandell and Pinder 2012: 5–6).

The settlers brought their political, religious and legal systems with them and established a European-like society in Canada (Harhoff 1993: 366–408). Unfortunately, they also brought 'the coloniser ideology' with them, which considers Indigenous People primitive and without any real civilisation in terms of law, art, trade, politics, crafts, agriculture, religion or ownership of land (Mandell 2015a: 1–8). From the late eighteenth century, but particularly in the late nineteenth and early twentieth centuries, the Canadian government and 'European Canadians' tried to delete what was considered the barbarian indigenous culture in order to bring civilisation to the savages (Harhoff 1993: 374–375).

The legal system proved a powerful tool in this process. Laws like the Gradual Civilization Act (1857) and the Indian Act (1876) were passed. These laws established reservations, where the Native Peoples had to live, and passed restrictions on eligibility to vote in band elections; they forbid traditional dress and the practising of dances, decreased hunting and fishing areas, forbid people to visit other groups in their reservation, banned traditional religious, legal and social practices such as the *Potlatch*, which functioned as a form of the 'Supreme Court' for the Indigenous Peoples; and they imposed severe sanctions on people not converting to Christianity, such as laws preventing non-Christians from testifying or having their cases heard in court (Mandell 2015a: 3; Mandell and Pinder 2012). Furthermore, from 1927 to 1951, the native voice of a legal challenge over land rights had been silenced by the Canadian government, as it was illegal for an Indigenous nation or person to raise money to take the land question to court—and for any lawyers to help them doing so (Mandell 2015a: 8). Laws, like the Royal Proclamation of 1763, protecting one's land rights are of little use, if one is forbidden by another law to raise a land question in the courts.

In other words, even though Canada's past and colonial history is less bloody than that of other places in the world, and even though it does hold examples of respectful cooperation over questions of land and resources between Indigenous Peoples and European-descendant Canadians, it is still a story unfolding deep harm and injustice and a 'master culture' living by the rule 'might is right' rather than by the rule of law. In many cases, the government and the provinces in Canada have not respected the rights of natives nor honoured the law (Harhoff 1993: 378–381). Instead, without permission and concluding treaties, their practice was to take control over the land and its resources of fishing, mining, farming and lumber production.

The paradigm of colonialism slowly shifted globally during the last part of the twentieth and the first part of twenty-first centuries. Indigenous Peoples in Canada, as in other parts of the world, gradually regained some of the right to be legal subjects with equal rights. Once that shift had reached the legal system, Native Peoples started going to the courts in order to claim justice and make governments and the surrounding societies respect native right to self-government and honour their title to land, laws, traditions, languages and religions. This also happened in Canada (Harhoff 1993: 410–411).

However, at the same time the political and legal process leading to Canada's independence from the UK in 1982 had begun, and here Indigenous Peoples were not invited nor allowed to take part in the negotiation process (Mandell and Pinder 2012). The Indigenous Peoples rightfully feared that one of the reasons for this was that politicians planned that the partition should entail an annihilation of Indigenous Peoples' title to land (Harhoff 1993: 400). For obvious practical, historical and financial reasons, the idea of 'aboriginal rights' was unpopular in many parts of the Canadian society (Mandell and Pinder 2012: 1–3). In order to be heard and to avoid the removal of natives' title to land from the new Canadian Constitution, legal and political action was taken by several Indigenous Peoples.

In 1977 the Union of BC Indian Chiefs hired the lawyers Louise Mandell and Leslie Pinder (Mandell 2015a: 8). Their task was to work together with the Chiefs for an entrenchment of Native Rights before the partition of Canada and the UK. Later the task transformed into taking the land question to court (Mandell and Pinder 2012: 1). Indigenous Peoples asserted that their sovereign rights and aboriginal title to land were valid and intact from the time before the Europeans first came to

Canada (Harhoff 1993: 370–373), and therefore they had title to much more land than the reservations, in which they had been placed by the government. Natives conceived the relationship with the UK Crown to be a partnership, and likewise the old numbered treaties and the Canadian Constitution of 1867 were conceived to express pacts among equal 'founding peoples' (Mandell and Pinder 2012: 4).

But even though the Native Peoples of Canada succeeded in bringing national and international political and media attention to their cause in the years up to the passing of *The Canadian Bill* and the final partition in 1982, they were never included in the negotiation process and the constitutional reform (Mandell and Pinder 2012: 8–16). What was managed to be saved of aboriginal title in the new Canadian Constitution of 1982 was sections 25 and 35, the latter which "recognizes and affirms the existing aboriginal rights" (Mandell and Pinder 2012: 16). But, not surprisingly, when it came to the questions of land rights, the insertion of section 35 in the Constitution, and especially how it was interpreted afterwards by both the Canadian courts and government, did not prove to be a happy ending. The government's practice of taking land without properly addressing native title continued and continues even to this day.[2] But at this point in history the Indigenous Peoples are no longer robbed of their legal voice, and for years, they have openly asked in court rooms, like the Haida:

> Where's the government's bill of sale? How did the government get title to the lands and waters, and the fish they claim to be able to destroy, when the Haida never surrendered our land? (Mandell 2015a: 1)

Over the past 40 years, these questions have been addressed through several landmark cases in the Canadian legal system.[3] During the court cases it became apparent that the 'colonial ideology' was still alive, not only in the political system, through the governmental practice of using land without properly addressing native title, but also in the legal system, in particular in the way section 35 of the Constitution and the term 'aboriginal rights' were interpreted by the courts.

[2] See, for instance, *Gitxaala Nation v. Canada* (2016, FCA 187).

[3] Precedent setting court cases have been *Calder v. Attorney-General of British Columbia* (1973), *Guerin v. The Queen* (1984), *The Queen v. Sparrow* (1990), *The Queen v. Van der Peet* (1996) and *The Queen v. Powley* (2003) (http://indigenousfoundations.arts.ubc.ca/home/land-rights.html; accessed 3.8.2016).

When Mandell and Pinder's firm ran cases for the Union of B.C. Indian Chiefs, they encountered and had to disprove or refute a large number of colonial legal doctrines and false claims about Indigenous Peoples' culture, legal system and uses of land[4]: Among these were Indigenous Peoples being primitive with no *real* law and political power, and certainly no effective power and control over their territories, nor had they special laws for the use of the land (the myth of *the juridical vacuum* and the colonial legal principle of *terra nullis*, a place without owner one is allowed to take ownership over); it was claimed that the land was unoccupied (the colonial *doctrine of discovery*); or if it was occupied, then only so in very small spots, like a fishing place or a farm; or if not just in small spots, then the land was only used for 'a nomadic roaming and passing through'. Likewise it was claimed that the natives had had no *real* concept of land ownership before the encounter with the European settlers; that the natives did not live by the rule of law, but more by custom, accordingly making it legitimate for the Crown to extinguish native title and rights and upheave treaties through legislation (the *extinguishment doctrine* and the *doctrine of parliamentary supremacy*); that Native Peoples did not act because of institutions, but only because of 'survival instincts that varied from village to village'; that if there is some kind of native title today, then prior to this being proven in court, natives have no right to be consulted or have their needs and interests in the land accommodated by the government and so forth (Mandell 2015a, b, 2014, 2012; Mandell and Pinder 2012).

The challenges in disproving and rejecting the above legal, ideological and factual claims were many, some of them typical for legal disputes, like establishing the facts of the case and how to interpret central terms, here 'aboriginal rights' and 'existing' in section 35 of the Constitution. Other challenges went right to the very heart of this particular dispute. This happened, for example, when the government and the lower courts could not accept *adaawk* (oral history), dirge songs, crests, totem poles, native accounts of their laws of stewardship, feast system, and use and management of their territories through generations *as evidence* of ancient territorial ownership (Mandell 2015a: 8; Mandell and Pinder 2012: 2–3). Here is Mandell's recollection:

[4] The cases *Delgamuukw v. British Columbia* (1997, 3 SCR 1010), *Haida Nation v. British Columbia (Minister of Forests)* (2004, SCC73), and *Tsilhqot'in v. British Columbia* (2014, SCC 44).

> We are about to enter an era where the issues of voice and entitlement to speak, as well as to be heard, are the dominant metaphors of the political discourse. Subsequently, this was perhaps best epitomized during the first lengthy test case on Aboriginal title in British Columbia. Mary Johnson, a Gitksan-Wet'suwet'en elder, was giving evidence of her adaawk (oral history), part of which was expressed in a dirge song. Despite the significance of the song showing ancient territorial ownership, the trial Judge didn't want to hear it. 'I have a tin ear,' Judge McEachern said. 'It's not going to do any good to sing to me'. Indeed, it didn't do any good. He ruled that Aboriginal title in B.C. had been extinguished. (Mandell and Pinder 2012: 3)

An elderly woman singing a traditional song did not make *sense* to the judges as an example of proof of land ownership. Perhaps it was even found ridiculous. It was something to be entirely dismissed as evidence. The government and courts also refused to recognise that Native Peoples have a different kind of concept of law and ownership than the settlers, and that they have another form of farming practice. To have a different kind is, clearly, not the same as not having a concept of law or land ownership or as not being farmers (Mandell 2012: 6–7).

Another problem was ignorance in the sense of lack of information: "One challenge was how little was known about Indigenous Peoples and their legal and political circumstances" (Mandell and Pinder 2012: 11). This is not surprising given it was a legal and political system that a physically superior power had attempted to erase for more than a hundred years. Yet, there was historical, archaeological and anthropological help to get, sometimes from surprising places—like an old indigenous straw hat found on a European museum—in order to disprove the false claims and give insight in the native laws and communities.

Still, the legal battle took many years—the *Delgamuukw* alone took 14 years, before the Supreme Court of Canada made a final judgement. Each time the result was a small step forward (Mandell 2014: 5; 2015a: 9; 2015b: 3). The Supreme Court's decisions over and again sent the same message to the Native Peoples, to the lower courts and to the political system; a message supported by the International Community in the form of the UN, who had condemned Canada's government's treatment of Indigenous Peoples several times. The message was "Canada's Aboriginal peoples were here when the Europeans came and were never conquered" (Mandell 2015b: 5). This translates to: Aboriginal title had never been extinguished, and it finds expression in the Constitution of 1982 (section

35), aboriginal title confers ownership rights, the title is not confirmed to small spots, oral history is admissible in native land questions as evidence on the same footing as historical record (Mandell 2014: 4; 2015a: 9; 2015b: 3). Governments and others seeking to use the land must—if they wish to follow the law and Supreme Court decisions and uphold the basic principle of the rule of law—therefore first clear the question of aboriginal title, and in case of such title, they need to obtain the consent of the title holders.

> Aboriginal title confers ownership rights over the territory [...], including the right to decide how the land will be used, enjoyment, occupancy, possession, economic benefits and the right to proactively use and manage. (Mandell 2014: 4)

The Supreme Court hereby also "placed reconciliation at the heart of the constitutional relationship" between Native Peoples and the government (Mandell 2015a: 9; 2014: 7). The idea is to resolve land questions through negotiations and consent between equal parties (Mandell 2014: 8). This can be seen as a way of re-establishing traditional indigenous legal culture focusing on decisions made by consensus (Harhoff 1993: 395, 397). These changes represent what Mandell sees as legal paradigm shift.

To make sense of the shift as a paradigm shift in Kuhn's sense of the word, we have to look for changes that incarnate a form of incommensurability (e.g. in values, in concepts, in ideals, what counts as fact and reality) between the old and the new paradigm, and I believe we can find that.[5] Before the legal paradigm shift, what in the Canadian courts counted as, for example, 'evidence', 'legally valid agreements', 'ownership', 'proof

[5] Kuhn (1970) introduces the idea of 'paradigm shifts' in the natural sciences. One of the things that characterises a paradigm shift is that there is 'incommensurability' between the paradigm before and the paradigm after a scientific revolution. What counts as 'good science', as 'measuring rod', as 'measuring', as 'criteria', as 'logical', 'as self-evidently true', as 'an investigation', as 'a fact' and so forth can mean something radically different before and after a shift of a paradigm. A paradigm shift entails "changes in the standards governing permissible problems, concepts, and explanations" (Kuhn 1970: 106). How Kuhn understood 'incommensurability', and if there is incommensurability between paradigms in such a strong sense as described here, is hotly debated to this day. The equivalent of this debate in moral philosophy will be addressed in Part II of the book. By accepting Mandell's use of the term 'paradigm change', I do not claim that the two legal paradigms—the colonial and the legal pluralistic—in the case discussed earlier cannot be compared in any meaningful ways. In this case (at least so far), the legal system has in most respects remained the same.

of ownership', 'a practice of farming' and 'a use of land' was something radically different. The Native Peoples would present what they considered to be valid evidence of ownership and use of land according to existing contracts, treatise and tradition—only to have it discarded and ignored because what was presented made no sense in the colonial paradigm as proofs. But after the paradigm shift all of the above could make sense as evidence and did count as such—the legal system had to some extent change its fundamental conception of what 'evidence', 'ownership', 'use of land' and 'farming' are. Thus, if a judge's 'ear is too thin' to hear a dire song today, he, not the proof, would need to be preplaced.

Another aspect of the legal paradigm shift is the courts' practice when interpreting the existing legal materials. The laws on the land question stayed the same before and after the paradigm shift, and Canada's legal system can be said to have been legal pluralistic since the days when the settlers arrived. But the court's practice of interpreting this pluralistic foundation has changed—from a practice of colonial interpretation (e.g. to ignore the native legal order) to a practice of truly legal pluralistic interpretation.

> The colonial paradigm shifted. The new paradigm [*sic*] is legal pluralism—the simultaneous existence of two legal orders, Crown and Indigenous [*sic*]—distinct spheres of authority emanating [*sic*] from different cultures, both having titles and jurisdiction, each arising from different sources, both governing and operating on the same landscape. (Mandell 2015a: 9)

Besides being a legal paradigm shift it also represents a major moral change affecting all Indigenous Peoples in Canada—after hundreds of years of cruel and unjust treatment, there is finally recognition and the possibility of a rebirth of justice.

The colonial legal paradigm was transformed by forces both in and outside Canada. Native Peoples chose to start cases, and the question of land rights got coverage from the international media. The Supreme Court began recognising the consequences of the fact that Indigenous Peoples were in the land before the settlers and that there were laws protecting Indigenous land-rights, hereby strengthening the foundation of legal pluralism, on which Canada was originally built. The Canadian government further passed laws giving political and legal rights back to

Indigenous Peoples.[6] In 1991 Canada ratified the UN *Convention 169 on Indigenous and Tribal Peoples.* On several occasions, the international political community, like the UN, put pressure on the Canadian government by strongly encouraging it to change its practice on native issues. And the UN created the *Declaration of the Rights of Indigenous Peoples* (adopted by the General Assembly 2007), which Canada originally voted against, but supports today.[7]

The ongoing journey towards a rebirth of justice for the Native Peoples of Canada can be told in the form of classical folk's tale: The heroine of the story starts out at home, but she is compelled or—as in this case—forced to leave her home and go on a dangerous and challenging journey, only in the end to return home; yet, the heroine, and often also the home, has been substantially changed during the process. Our native heroine is thus not returning to a legal order of the form before the arrival of the settlers to her homeland. What she arrives at is something new. What still needs to be changed to have justice fully reborn is among other things that the political practice of using land without prior permission—or, put more bluntly, the practice of stealing—is stopped.[8]

[6] For example, Bill C-31 passed in 1985, and *The Aboriginal Right to Self-Government Policy* in 1995.

[7] https://www.un.org/development/desa/indigenouspeoples/declaration-on-the-rights-of-indigenous-peoples.html.

[8] I thank Professor Lear for bringing to my attention the example of the Canadian Indigenous Peoples' legal fight for land rights and for putting me in touch with lawyer Louise Mandell (http://www.mandellpinder.com). I also thank Mandell for supplying me with the majority of the sources for this section (her various reading notes for meetings with her clients) and her comments on the section. As I am neither a lawyer nor a historian and as the point of the story is to be a philosophical tool, the narrative in this section most likely has flaws and imprecisions in both legal and historical respect, flaws for which I have full responsibility.

CHAPTER 6

# Poor Little Sweep! Child Labour in the UK

> After passing through the Chimney and descending to the second angle in the fire-place, the Boy finds it completely filled with soot, which he has dislodged from the sides of the upright part. He endevours to get through, and succeeds in doing so, after much struggling as far as his shoulders; but finding that the soot is compressed hard all around him, by his exertions, that he can recede no farther; he then endevours to move forward, but his attempts in this respect are quite abortive; for the covering of the horizontal part of the Flue being stone, the sharp angle of which bears hard on his shoulders, and the back part of his head … prevents him from moving in the least either one way or the other. His face, already covered with a climbing cap, and being pressed hard in the soot beneath him, stops his breath. In this dreadful condition he strives violently to extricate himself, but his strength fails him; he cries and groans, and in a few minutes he is suffocated. An alarm is then given, a brick-layer is sent for, an aperture is perforated in the Flue, and the boy is extracted, but found lifeless. In a short time an inquest is held, and a Coroner's Jury returns a verdict of 'Accidental Death'. (Waldron 1983: 391)

From late eighteenth century and onwards, the idea of the child as innocent and the ideal of a childhood devoted to education and play, which had originated among artists and philosophers in the Enlightenment and Romantic period, now became more widespread in the upper and steadily growing middle classes in the West (Fass 2013: 7). Industrialisation and urbanisation had led to increased wealth in many societies. With more wealth and as a result of that freedom from work for an increasing number


C. Eriksen, *Moral Change*,
https://doi.org/10.1007/978-3-030-61037-1_6

of children, it was possible for well-off parents to live up to the ideal of giving their children a childhood with education and play.

> Beginning in the eighteenth century, children gradually no longer had to do heavy work [...], and subsequently children were excluded from adult life. They could be free to play, to learn and to explore, as Rousseau envisaged. (Koren 1996: 139, 141)

However, the contrasts between this new ideal of childhood, the lives of children of the privileged classes and the lives of children in the working class in the industrialised cities, were striking, and it was found increasingly disturbing and revolting by people in the elite and middle classes (Morrison 2012: 115–117, 334). Children, especially orphans and very poor children, sometimes as young as three to four years of age, were still put to hard work (Cunningham 2012: 361; Fass 2013: 4). And even though children had always done work in agriculture and as servants and apprentices, the industrialisation changed their working conditions completely. These children were not well-fed, not appropriately dressed, and did not receive proper treatment when sick. Their workday could be between 10–16 hours and their working week 6–7 days. Furthermore, children more often than adults worked under extremely dangerous conditions, when employed underground in mines, in cotton factories, and cleaning chimneys (Cunningham 2012: 361–365; Mayhew 1967). In other words, the industrialisation witnessed what we today would label a massive exploitation of poor and orphaned children.

This exploitation was mainly possible due to the intact ancient tradition for child work: massive poverty combined with the fact that under the industrialisation there was a strong demand for their small sizes as well as cheap, or even free, labour. Employing children, instead of their parents, helped produce cheaper commodities, which gave the owner of a factory or store an advantage on the market. That 'sons took the work of fathers' happened for factory workers in the textile industry, as well as for woodworkers and boot and shoemakers (Cunningham 2012: 363–364; Grahn-Farley 2013: 36). In combination, these factors created very harsh working conditions for unprivileged children. The mines, the factories and the chimneys became paradigm cases in changing the public's view on child labour and creating a demand for laws regulating the area. There had been laws regulating the area of child labour before this, aimed at work as servants or apprentices. The novelty in this period was thus not laws regulating child labour, but the first voicing of the assertion that children had a right not to work at all (Cunningham 2012: 361), combined with the much stricter laws on child labour.

Children were used as chimney sweeps because of their sizes. The chimneys were at this time long, pitch-black, filled with ash, soot and creosote, and very narrow. In houses with several storages a chimney could extend upwards 60 feet or more and would typically have many corners, turns and twists to accommodate living space, and because it was often attached to other flues within the building to share a chimney opening.[1] Children would get stuck or lost in the pipes, suffocating or burning to death, as it was recounted above by a sweep witnessing the fate of one chimney boy. These so-called accidental deaths, however, were not the only occupational hazards that child chimney sweeps suffered:

> In the 1817 report to [the UK] Parliament, witnesses reported that climbing boys suffered from general neglect, and exhibited stunted growth and deformity of the spine, legs and arms, which were thought to be caused by being required to remain in abnormal positions for long periods of time before their bones had hardened. The knees and ankle joints were the most affected. Sores and inflammation of the eyelids that could lead to loss of sight, were slow in healing because the boy kept rubbing them. Bruises and burns were obvious hazards of having to work in an overheated environment. Cancer of the scrotum was found only in chimney sweeps so was referred to as Chimney Sweep Cancer in the teaching hospitals. Asthma and inflammation of the chest were attributed to the fact that the boys were out in all weathers.[2]

Not only an increase in wealth but also art proved to be powerful ally of working children. In 1785, an English mercantilist, Jonas Hanway, wrote a book about the lives of chimney children, *A Sentimental History of Chimney Sweepers*, which moved his contemporaries deeply and motivated them to lobby for a change in the laws on child labour. The book initiated a whole genre of poems and literature drawing attention to the conditions of the poor and working-class children (Cunningham 2012: 262). The artistic atmosphere of the time surrounding working children is condensed

[1] https://owlcation.com/humanities/The-History-of-Children-at-Work-The-Poor-Life-of-An-Apprentice-Chimney-Sweep (accessed 15.7.2017).

[2] https://en.wikipedia.org/wiki/Chimney_sweep (accessed 04.06.2020).

in the first four lines of William Blake's poem 'The Chimney Sweeper' from *Songs of Innocence*, first published in 1789.

> When my mother died I was very young,
> And my father sold me while yet my tongue.
> Could scarcely cry "'weep! 'weep! 'weep! 'weep!"
> So your chimneys I sweep & in soot I sleep.

A further mobilising effect on the public and politicians could be seen from the reports made by the UK government on the working conditions of children, like *Report from the Committee of the honourable the House of Commons on the Employment of Boys in Sweeping of Chimneys* from 1817 and *The Physical and Moral Condition of the Children and Young Persons Employed in Mines and Manufactures* from 1843. The reports investigated the working conditions of children working in mines and factories in England, Ireland, Scotland and Wales. Politicians and the public were shocked by the reports, which contained oral testimony sometimes 'from children as young as five'.[3] Some of these reports also contained drawings showing (thus not only reporting about) the working conditions to the politicians, and through reproduction in newspapers also showing them to the rest of the public.[4]

All of this led to a demand for laws protecting children (Morrison 2012: 115–117).[5] "The early legislation controlling the employment of children in factories and mines was conspicuously motivated by a wish to protect the interests of children" (Eekelaar 1986: 167). In the nineteenth century the UK government passed child labour laws to protect working children, for instance, by banning children under the age of nine from working in factories and restricting the hours of children under the age of 14 to eight hours a day. The act was backed by an inspection to make sure that the laws were kept (Cunningham 2012: 362–364). Such legislative efforts to protect children against work—as well as other kinds of harm, like neglect, physical and sexual assault, incest and murder—took place all over the West (McGillivray 2011: 27).

[3] http://www.bl.uk/collection-items/the-physical-and-moral-condition-of-the-children-and-young-persons-employed-in-mines-and-manufactures-1843 (accessed 15.7.2017).

[4] An example can be seen here: https://www.bl.uk/collection-items/report-on-child-labour-1842 (accessed 19.7.2017).

[5] Often the women's movement is also considered a significant factor in improving the legal status of children in the West (Grahn-Farley 2013: 20; Koren 1996: 143).

For thousands of years the often extreme physical, social and psychological abuse and sufferings of some groups of children had existed in plain sight, but it was only from the mid-1800s and onwards that it was believed that these sufferings were unacceptable and that the government (and not only private persons and the church) had a moral obligation to deal with them. Earlier, people talked about, for instance, orphans and children born out of wedlock as problems, because they were seen as causing a disturbance in the public order (Dübeck 2013: 66–70), and for that reason the government had an obligation to deal with them. But their *sufferings* had not been considered a cause for public outrage or a reason for a lot of political action. That connection was not made. So, what explains this sudden seeing and caring for suffering, which had always been there to see in plain sight?

There does not seem to be a simple explanation for this moral change and thus not one main factor to point to as the most important or triggering dynamic. The spread of wealth may have allowed the middle class to see and act on the suffering, because they could afford to do so, with no great cost to themselves, unlike the chimney colleague to the boy we encountered in the introduction. Speaking up against the cruel treatment of the chimney boys would most likely cost him his job—and as a consequence perhaps sending his own children into the streets. The spread of the new ideal of childhood can be seen as another reason why the politicians and the politically influential classes were confronting themselves with the horrible working condition of poor children, as they did through their reading of novels, newspapers and government reports. Lynn Hunt have shown that novels are able to create identification and solidarity between the reader and the hero of the book, even though the hero is living a life either socially or physically remote from the reader (Hunt 2008). Hanway's book was successful in doing so, as it not only set forth the dry facts of the cruelties of child work, but did so in a rhetoric creating emotions and solidarity. Through the story, Hanway let his privileged readers meet the poor children and their lives close up, allowing for sympathy to arise. He further appealed to the moral values of the upper and middle classes through concepts like humanity, Christianity, pity, compassion, national honour and tradition and linked them to the lives of poor children (Cunningham 2012). The fact that people from the elite and middle classes would spend their time reading and writing books on children in the working class and were moved to political lobbying on behalf of them shows that the new ideal of childhood was conceived to apply to *all* children, not just the privileged ones. Accordingly, wealthy people conceived it as their moral duty to do something to better the lives of these children.

Earlier in history it had not made the same kind of sense to compare and draw connections between the life of a rich and the life of a poor child because they naturally belonged to entirely different spheres of existence, with different rules and values applying; not unlike how human and animal lives today are seen as belonging to two different spheres of existence, with different rules and values applying. The new universal ideal of childhood created the connection and made it meaningful to compare the rich and the poor child in new ways, to draw connections between what was formerly unrelated lives. The moral ideal, developed in the Enlightenment and Romantic period, thus gave adults in the West a new way of raising their children and gave children other things to do—to go to school instead of going to work in the fields and factories.[6]

> The clearest transformation in childhood's world history involves the replacement of agricultural with industrial societies (and the imitation of industrial patterns, like mass schooling, even in societies still striving to complete the industrialization process). Not everything changed, of course [...]—but the basic purpose of childhood was redefined. (Stearns 2006: 6)

What happens from late 1700 to 1900 is that the conception of the child moves from being an object in the sense of being the property of the family or father to becoming 'an object of care' with a right to wellbeing and thus to be protected by parents and employers, and if they were not up to the task, by the state (Koren 1996: 141). Legally and morally, there was a shift of emphasis from employer's and parents' rights and interests to the child's welfare and best interest (Van Buren 1995: xxi; McGillivray 2011: 29).

Yet, while new ideals of childhood, wealth, art and knowledge induced a wish and gave the ability to take better care of poor working children, these were not the only dynamics behind the changes of the legal systems

[6] Morrison interestingly notes that imperialism and colonisation, understood as the time between the fifteenth and twentieth centuries, often worked to move childhood of non-western children in the opposite direction from 'the modern model'—by actively seeking to keep indigenous children out of school and instead increasing these children's participation in the labour force (Morrison 2012: 117–118).

of the West during this period. Politically, childhood and children also came increasingly into focus because of a decline in birth rates, a still high infant mortality rate, a need for soldiers, and an idea of the importance of moulding the right kind of citizen for democratic national states, which became one of the main goals of the practice of schooling. Fear of communism also played an important role in the Western countries, as well as a fear of delinquent children threatening social cohesion, still was a motive when it came to politicians' wish to take better care of children (see, e.g. Eekelaar 1986: 168; Cunningham 2012: 359; Fass 2013: 3–7; Grahn-Farley 2013: 1–145).

The aforementioned narrative can be seen as a story of moral progress where the life quality of large groups of poor and working children went from bad to better. It can also be seen as narrative of moral change in the sense that a society changed its conception of who has a right to live 'a good life'. The conception of childhood and ideal of childhood as an innocent life period dedicated to education and play did not change in this period, but the conception of who this ideal applied to changed—its scope was broadened. On the level of social morality, this is thus a case of moral reform, as the change in societal morality was brought about by the active work of various agents (artists, citizens, politicians, etc.), but not a moral revolution, as, for instance, the basic moral ideas, values and ideals were not changed (Baker 2019: 17–51, 195–213).

CHAPTER 7

# From Death Penalty to Church Weddings

> Homosexuality was deemed among other things: Contrary to the will of God, unnatural and a source of social disintegration. And during those centuries the legal treatment of homosexuals reflected this moral/religious understanding, wherefore homosexuality was classified as a very severe offence often punished by death. (Viskum 2015: 62)

Denmark's record of maltreating homosexuals is long and dark, as it is in many other countries. Even after the secularisation had loosened the church's tight grip on public morality, and the laws no longer prescribed death sentences, homosexuality was still illegal and something strongly socially stigmatising both for the individual and her or his family. In Denmark, homosexuality was considered a crime until 1933, and a diagnosable disease in the psychiatric system until 1980 (Ibid.).[1]

The first change in the Danish government's treatment of homosexuals was decriminalisation. This was the result of three things mainly (Ibid.: 62–66): Firstly, a rise in the political and legal system of liberal values; secondly, the political valuation and strengthening of a distinction between the private and the public spheres, where the state should mainly deal with the public sphere, while sexuality was deemed to belong to the private

[1] The change described in this section is not unique to Denmark. It has happened in most of Europe and Northern America during a fairly similar time period with varying courses. For example, see Baker (2019: 43–49) for a short narrative of the gay movement in the USA.


C. Eriksen, *Moral Change*,
https://doi.org/10.1007/978-3-030-61037-1_7

sphere; and lastly, the spread of a concept of individual rights. "In the end it was the [legislators'] commitment to a consistent application of liberal values rather than a positive moral evaluation of homosexuality that motivated the decriminalization" (Ibid.: 64). The rule of law works as a basic ideal of justice in modern legal systems in democratic societies. This ideal entails the legal principle of consistency—including treating like-cases alike, unless there are good reasons for not doing so.

The political commitment to liberal values and the principle of consistency led to a legal change with great moral impact for homosexuals and their relatives, as the decriminalisation to some extent normalised homosexuality and allowed homosexuals to openly have partners and live without fear of legal sanctions. When people in Denmark and other parts of Europe more openly and extensively could live as homosexuals, including buying a home and raising kids together, homosexuals began having new needs, equal to the needs of heterosexuals—but the latter group had official legal measures to help them cover these needs. This was, for instance, the need to be able to secure their partner and kids financially in the case of their death. This new need led to the use of lawyers and legal contracts:

> Citizens, professions and the business world often develop new norms in response to new situations or changing moral opinions. They may use contracts to formulate them. For example, before states formally recognized marriages or partnerships between same-sex couples, lawyers had been drafting cohabitation contracts for many years. (Van Der Burg 2014: 122–123)

At the end of the twentieth century, the moral views of most people in Denmark and in many other European countries had changed into an acceptance of homosexuality as a normal and natural form of sexuality (Viskum 2015: 66). This acceptance came about because of the decriminalisation, and further because when homosexuals lived openly together, it became obvious that they were not 'perverted and sick' people undermining society. On the contrary they were to the same degree as the rest of the population average people, responsible citizens and caring parents.

As the majority came to accept homosexuality, and gay people could live with dignity, pressure was also put on the legal system 'to catch up', a pressure, mainly coming from homosexuals, but it was supported by large parts of the Danish population (Ibid.: 66). The pressure stemmed from the remaining lack of equal rights. It is one thing for a human to enjoy 'negative freedom' (like the freedom from criminalisation, stigmatisation and harassment), and another thing also to enjoy 'positive freedom' and full legal and moral recognition (the freedom to do the same things as other adult members of one's community—like getting married, adopting children, getting an insemination, and being both openly gay and a honoured official ambassador for one's country). Besides the pressure on the political and legal system from homosexuals and the population, there was also a remaining internal pressure in the legal and political system out of respect for the rule of law and the principle of consistency: if homosexuality was not harmful, why should same-sex couple not enjoy equal rights with heterosexual couples—like the right to marriage? There was no good reason to deny them this within the frame of liberal values (Ibid.: 65). This resulted in several further legal changes in Denmark, like the enactment of civil union laws for same-sex couples in 1989, an artificial insemination law from 2006, and the church union laws in 2012. The result is that today Denmark is the country in the world closest to full legal recognition of homosexual people (Ibid.: 63).

What drove and created this change was first the political wish to adhere to liberal values and a principle of coherence and later it was joined by the homosexuals', the public's and the politicians' wish and work to obtain equality. The dynamics displayed in this story of a moral change can be described as a positive feedback-mechanism between law and ethics, and it shows that morally, "law sometimes leads and sometimes follows" (Green 2013a: 486). That is sometimes passing laws will create moral change, and at other times our moral values changes, and that leads us to change the laws. The legal adherence to an ideal of the rule of law and the legal principle of equity and a political commitment to liberal values lead to a legal change, which has the side-effect of enhancing the rights of homosexuals as the aim was not so much to do good for homosexuals, but to adhere to the principle. This change had moral consequences as it created the possibility of a significantly better and more dignified life for homosexuals. When homosexuals made use of the new possibilities the law gave them, this along with the decriminalisation (i.e. the political signal saying homosexuality is not harmful) led to a change of 'the public morality' in Denmark—how homosexuals were perceived and treated in ordinary life. But during this change the law ended up being 'morally behind' the moral values of the people, as politicians had not yet awarded full legal recognition and equal rights to homosexuals. The laws were conceived as unjust—it was discriminating and not a justifiably unequal treatment. The public therefore put pressure on the politicians for more legal changes. The politicians responded to the demands and passed new laws, this time with both the aim and effect of giving equal rights to homosexuals.

The moral changes displayed here are firstly, that the living conditions and quality of life of a group of people is bettered—in slogan form: from death penalty to church weddings. Secondly, on the level of societal morality, the change is that a form of sexuality goes from being considered morally bad (perverse, undermining society, harmful, etc.) to having a neutral value—it is now by the majority of people in Denmark considered a natural and harmless form of sexuality.

CHAPTER 8

# Being Moved Beyond Our Good and Evil: The Crow Case

> What if something *really unheard-of* happened?—If I, say, saw houses gradually turning into steam without any obvious cause; if the cattle in the fields stood on their heads and laughed and spoke comprehensible words; if trees gradually changed into men and men into trees. Now, was I right when I said before all these things happened "I know that that's a house" etc., or simply "that's a house" etc.? (Wittgenstein 2016: § 513)

Wittgenstein describes this mad Hieronymus Bosch world as part of an investigation of the concepts of knowledge and justification. Human history has never seen a change in reality as radical as this, though we do encounter it in films (*Annihilation*), paintings (Dali), literature (Kafka) and in discomforting dreams at night. However, the indigenous Canadians' land rights cases pointed to examples of encompassing and often rapid transformations in the form of life of a people, which history has witnessed a number of times, namely, the changes a people and their culture undergo when colonised. From ca. 1800 to 1900, the Native American tribe, the Crow, underwent such a radical change in what has been described as 'a cultural devastation' of their way of life (Lear 2008).[1]

A way of life exhibits a certain *form*—in the sense that over time, for instance, traditions and practices are upheld, fairly stable social roles are established, and certain rituals and ceremonial customs are repeatedly

[1] The following is referencing Lear's book *Radical Hope* (2008).


C. Eriksen, *Moral Change*,
https://doi.org/10.1007/978-3-030-61037-1_8

performed. Part of this form can also be a common overreaching *telos*, an understanding of what life is about, and what one should strive for in order to live an excellent life (Lear 2008: 55, 92).[2] Such telos provides a range of moral values, ideals and measuring rods for peoples' lives, and it gives meaning to their everyday doings. This was also the case for the Crow before 1800. What Crow life was about was essentially two things: Hunting and war.

> Fighting battles, defending one's territory, preparing to go to war—all this permeated the Crow way of life. [...] 'War was not the concern of a class nor even of the male sex, but of the whole population, from cradle to grave.' [...] everything was somehow related to hunting and war. All the rituals and customs, all the distribution of honor, all the day-to-day preparations, all the upbringing of the children were organized toward these ends. The flourishing life for the Crow was one of unfettered hunting of beaver and buffalo. (Lear 2008: 11, 12, 35–36)

However, this did not last. The Crow lands were taken over by a military superior power, in the form of the invading, colonising Europeans. The consequences were devastating. It amounted to "the death of a traditional way of life" (Lear 2008: 96). There could be no more warfare and no more travelling the lands as nomads, as the government forbade both practices, and during the period 1882–1884, the Crow moved to a reservation. There could be no more hunting for a living, as the invaders had killed all the game. The chief of the Crow during this transition, Chief Plenty Coups, recounts: "When the buffalo went away the hearts of my people fell to the ground, and they could not lift them up again. After this nothing happened" (Lear 2008: 2). *Nothing happened*—there were no great hunts or wars to prepare and celebrate. In the reservation, the Crow stopped their traditional ceremonies, like the Sun dance, as this ritual had ceased to make sense in the new setting. Acts, which formerly were associated with honour for young men aspiring to be great warriors, like conquering horses from the Sioux Indians, also took on another meaning in the new context, namely as dishonourable acts of stealing (Lear 2008: 27–28). The loss of meaning went to the very core of Crow life and

[2] A large part of Kierkegaard's pseudonymous works can be seen as giving voice to and describing different forms of life, with different *teloi* and meanings, within one society and culture.

permeated every aspect of it. All members of the tribe suffered massive disorientation. They did not know their way around in life anymore:

> Even with the collapse of the nomadic way of life, there were still meals to cook; there were still families that needed support. Yet in the written records of women's experiences there is also expression of confusion. [...] People continued to act practically, but they lost the rich framework in which such acts made sense. (Lear 2008: 60, 57)

The overall conception of the good life and almost all concepts, values and ideals, which had given meaning and direction to everything in their lives, had gone out of existence. They kept on living, but no longer had any clear idea as to *why* they were living, what living *well* could amount to, and what they had to raise their children *for* (Lear 2008: 57, 61). In this situation, there was a massive confusion in the tribe, and a lot of it was social, moral and conceptual. What does being brave entail in this new life? What is a meaningful sense of honourable fighting in this new context? Clarifying the meaning of the concepts in the Crow language would have been of little help, as these concepts found no application in the new world that the Crow found themselves in (Lear 2008: 65). To a large extent, the Crow had been moved 'beyond their good and evil' by forces and dynamics they had no or only limited control of. And they had not yet developed a new *telos*, new ideals, and new concepts to navigate in the world: "The tribe's problem was not just that they did not know what the future had in store; they lacked the concepts with which to experience it. [...] the Crow faced a challenge to all aspects of their lives." (Lear 2008: 78).

In the Crow case the political, geographical, biological and social preconditions for a form of life, which was about warfare and hunting, crumbled, and with that the Crow's form of life and morality crumbled too, to a great extent leaving them in a despairing conceptual, existential and moral void. These moral changes were involuntarily and forced upon them by the actions of a superior military power and the changes in their social and physical environment. Yet, the Crow still had to live and figure out what living well meant in these radically changed conditions. One of the moral challenges the Crow and their leaders were facing was how to cooperate with the enemy-government in a dignified way (the Crow could also have chosen not to co-operate but to wage continued war, as the case of the Sioux will underline in Part II). Transformations of the virtue of courage and the concept of honour had to be developed in order for this to happen. Important resources for this were found in their religion.

The Crow had an elaborate religious faith, religious practices and rich myths. According to Lear, their religious faith entailed 'a bedrock of hope'. To have a bedrock of hope in one's life is to have a form of basic trust that things will work out eventually, because the Gods are good and wish the best for us: "the fundamental goodness of the world is secure" (Lear 2008: 134), and it is secure even in the midst of total destruction. This faith helped the tribe and its leaders avoid despair; at least some of them some of the time. The Crow's religious faith also entailed an understanding of themselves as having a limited capacity for understanding what the good is. The Crow manifested:

> a commitment to the idea that the goodness of the world transcends one's limited and vulnerable attempts to understand it. [...] commitment to the idea that something good will emerge even if it outstrips my present limited capacity for understanding what that good is. [...] that while we Crow must abandon the goods associated with our way of life [...] *We shall get the good back,* though at the moment we can have no more than a glimmer of what that might mean. (Lear 2008: 95, 94)

Besides 'a bedrock of hope' and 'a limited understanding of what the good is', the Crow also had a practice of 'vision' or 'dream seeking'. The young members of the tribe, typically boys, were encouraged to go out in the nature to receive a vision from the Gods. The child would spend time alone and dream. Upon returning to the tribe, the elders would gather and interpret the dream-message from the Gods. "The tribe relied on what it took to be the young men's capacity to receive the world's imaginative messages; it relied on the old men to say what these messages meant" (Lear 2008: 71).

A dream dreamt by a nine-year-old boy, the boy who grew up to be Chief Plenty Coups, delivered a dream-narrative crucial in helping the Crow navigate through the destruction of their form of life. "Young Plenty Coups's dream [...] did not predict any particular event, but the change of the world order" (Lear 2008: 68). The dream was interpreted by the elders to predict the destruction of life, as the Crow knew it and to contain a hope and a way of surviving: It predicted that the white man would take and hold their country; it predicted the total extinction of the buffalo and its replacement by a buffalo-like animal from another world with a longer tail and various colours, some white with spots; it predicted that Plenty Coups would grow old; and it predicted a tremendous storm which would knock down all trees of countless Bird-people. All but one—the tree of the Chickadee. In the dream, a voice tells young Plenty Coups:

> [The Chickadee] is least in strength but strongest of mind among his kind. He is willing to work for wisdom. The Chickadee-person is a good listener. [... He] never misses a change to learn from others. He gains successes and avoids failure by learning how others succeeded or failed [...] Develop your body, but do not neglect your mind Plenty-coups. It is the mind that leads a man to power, not strength of body. (Lear 2008: 70–71)

Plenty Coups' dream was surreal, perceptive, scary, complex and ethically ripe, not unlike a Bosch painting. When wisely interpreted it contained useful information on a great many things, entailing how to transform the warrior's conception of strength into the kind of strength required in diplomacy and politics; skills strongly needed when the tribe had to fight to keep their lands through negotiations with the government. The dream provided the Crow with creative resources and a dignified path through the radical moral change they were going through. "The elders interpreted the dream to mean that if they followed the example of the chickadee, they would hold onto their lands. But what *holding onto their lands* would come to mean by say, 1955, was not something anyone could have imagined at the time of the dream, a hundred years earlier" (Lear 2008: 79). Plenty Coups's dream drew upon traditional mythological stories of the Crow (Lear 2008: 139). The Chickadee has long been a figure respected among the Crow, though it did not seem to be the most central mythological figure. Now it was put to a new use.

The colonisation inflicted massive suffering and traumatic losses for the Crow, but they managed to survive to this day as a tribe and they did manage to hold on to larger areas of their land than many other tribes did. They also found ways of giving re-birth to what it means to be Crow. The ritual of the sun dance was, for instance, reintroduced in 1941—now organised around heartfelt requests, like the survival of a young girl going through heart surgery (Lear 2008: 152).

The main dynamics displayed in this narrative are the colonisation powers and the social, religious and political resourcefulness of the Crow tribe. Some of the moral changes the narrative bears witness to are the transformation of the virtue of courage and the meaning of concepts that play a morally central role in Crow life, such as 'strength' and 'honour'. This is connected to the overall transformation of life telos, the Crow life underwent, something I will return to in Part II. The colonisation further entailed changes in social and legal status for the tribe members, which can be categorised as moral and social regress. Before the colonisation, the Crow lived in a land where they were respected, even by their enemies. After the colonisation, just in virtue of being Native Americans, they inhabited a low status position in the American society and were oppressed in countless ways; something which to this day is not fully mended.

CHAPTER 9

# Co-work and Compromises: The Birth of the *CRC*

> It was getting late, and soon the evening routines of her home would set in. She held tight on to her pen, still new to writing and carefully formed word after word. It was a newspaper article for *Maly Przeglad*, The Little Review. Her father had promised they could send it in tomorrow. The envelope, all sharp lines and thick paper, lay ready next to her and radiated seriousness. She wanted to finish today. It was important. Something had to be done! A *barbed wire* had been set up around her favorite playground in Ogród Krasińskich.[1]

The *Universal Declaration of Human Rights* (UDHR) assigns its rights to all members of the human race (UDHR 1948: Preamble). Therefore, rights are also assigned to children. Unless they are explicitly excluded, which they are in some instances. Or unless the rights are implicitly understood to require qualification, like a minimum age in the case of the right to vote, marry, serve in armed forces or choose a religion (Brett 2012: 243; Archard 2015: 23). In the late 1970s, there was an increasing dissatisfaction with how UDHR and other international declarations addressing children in reality failed to protect the rights of children.

Poland had a long tradition of children's rights and was the first country to suggest that the UN should adopt a convention specifically on the

[1] Inspiration: https://culture.pl/en/article/maly-przeglad-a-little-review-with-a-big-impact (accessed 10.5.2019).



C. Eriksen, *Moral Change*,
https://doi.org/10.1007/978-3-030-61037-1_9

rights of the child (Van Buren 1995: 13; Freeman 2012: 3). There was general agreement in the UN that it was a good idea with a convention in order to give some increased legal force to the idea of children's rights.[2] It was also considered wise to work out a new legal document, due firstly to some of the problems that have appeared since 1959, when the last declaration on children was made. Secondly, this would also allow the newly decolonised nations and states, which had not been part of the 1959 drafting process, to become part of the drafting process of the convention (Grahn-Farley 2013: 265).

The dissatisfaction with the former international legal instruments had two main sources. One was that they did not sufficiently protect children from violence and suffering. When children are secured human rights through their parents as parental rights, as was the case with former international legal instruments, they lose protection when orphaned, when separated from parents in times of war, when fleeing unaccompanied by parents from war and military recruitment, and when their parents abuse them (Koren 1996: 151–186). In many countries of the world, there were "serious abuses of state and parental power, which prevailing [legal] arrangements patently could not stop" (Marks and Clapham 2005: 20). For instance, even though children in the so-called developed countries were no longer exploited, deformed and killed in the workforce, children were still so in other parts of the world. Furthermore, babies and children are biologically less capable than adults of enduring and surviving diseases, hunger and separation from family and caretakers (Archard 2015: 20; Van Buren 1995: 7–12). Children are not only physically more vulnerable than grown-ups, they are mentally so, too. Their natural trust, dependency and

[2]Within the UN system the term '*convention*' means 'formal multilateral treaties with a broad number of parties'. '*Declarations*', on the other hand, are not formal agreements; but rather statements of 'understanding of some matter or as to the interpretation of a particular provision'. A '*treaty*' is defined by the Vienna Convention on the Law of Treaties as 'an international agreement concluded between States in written form and governed by international law' (Grahn-Farley 2013: 244). Accordingly, a convention is a legally binding agreement (Nickel 2007: 15–16), while a declaration is an expression of an intention, with some moral weight. For further descriptions of the international legal human rights system, see Moeckli et al. (eds.) (2014); Krause and Scheinen (2012); Marks and Clapham (2005); For works with particular focus on children's rights, see Van Buren (1995); Freeman (2012); Freeman (ed.) (2004); Archard (2014); and Koren (1996). *The Convention of the Rights of the Child* (CRC) had international legal predecessors in the form of declarations, like the League of Nations' *The Geneva Declaration of the Rights of the Child* from 1924 and the UN *Declaration of the Rights of the Child* adopted in 1959 (CRC: Preamble).

intellectual capacities make them easy targets of abuse—like prostitution, harmful child labour, rape and use as child soldiers (Grahn-Farley 2013: 268–269). Further, a world report on violence against children documented "not only the prevalence of violence against children but that it exists in all countries, cutting across culture, class, education, income and ethnic origin" (Brett 2012: 262). In other words, despite their already firmly established 'caretaker aims', the existing international laws failed to protect and take sufficiently care of what was phrased 'the special needs of children' (Morrison 2012: 334: Ishay 2008: 304).

The other major source of dissatisfaction with the existing international legal instruments was that they failed to take care not only of children's special needs but also of their capacity for agency. From the 1940s to the present day, the image of the child and the ideal of childhood have once again changed in the culture and legal systems of the Western countries (McGillivray 2011: 24; Marks and Clapham 2005: 20). The images of the Enlightenment and the Romantic period of the child in need of care and the ideal of childhood as a period devoted to school and play were not replaced, but supplemented. What was new was the view of children as agents competent to make their own decisions (Stephens 2012: 388; Koren 1996: 143–149).[3]

The view of the child as capable of making its own decision was closely linked to the experiences of Second World War and the Cold War. The governments of democratic countries, like Sweden and the USA, found it important that children were raised and trained as democratic citizens in order to counter the threat of Nazism and fascism in Europe and communism in the Soviet (Grahn-Farley 2013: 143). The ideals of democracy entail not only that children gain a historical and theoretical knowledge of democracy, but also that they learn to participate in a democracy and hence master the practical and social skills of being a democratic citizen. Children were seen to have a right to a voice equal to adults in order for them to learn to be active citizens in a democracy: learn the art of being heard, of listening, arguing their case, respecting different opinions, making compromises, cooperating despite differences, negotiating—in other words be taught to participate in the government of their country (Grahn-Farley 2013: 87, 111). This need to spread and safeguard the social and

[3] Landmark cases were *Tinker v. Des Moines Independent Community School District* 393 U.S. 503 (1969); *Gillick v West Norfolk & Wisbeck Area Health Authority* [1986] AC 112 House of Lords.

political skills of democratic citizenship was seen not only as an important agenda nationally but also internationally. In the USA "there were a strong push toward the internationalization of the child and youth export of democratic values" (Grahn-Farley 2013: 143).

This was the main background leading to the UN in 1979 decided to create a new international legal instrument aiming at better securing the human rights of children, which meant all human beings below the age of 18 years (CRC, Part 1, § 1). "The starting point for a consideration of the human rights of children is the insight that children are both the same as adults and different from them" (Brett 2012: 243), which is what merits a separate convention for them (Van Buren 1995: 9–13). The political drafting process leading to it was in many ways remarkable in international politics and exemplary of the possibility of accomplishing its democratic aims (Alston 2004: 183). Here Koren tells the story of the birth of the *Convention of the Rights of the Child* (CRC):

> The drafting process took ten years, showing some characteristics which have seldom been observed in international settings. To mention some of these, the open-ended nature of the Working Group implied that any of the forty-three states represented on the UN Commission on Human Rights could participate. All other member states and international organisations could send observers, which even could take the floor. NGO's in consultative status with the UN Economic and Social Council were also welcome but had no absolute right to speak. During the drafting process, these NGO's started to form a group, which prepared in advance alternative texts and amendments to the draft. Although these organisations had very different backgrounds, they were all involved in work with and for children and concerned with their rights. Their work was appreciated by the governmental delegates, which frequently used their experiences and proposals. Meetings were held in public. [...] the Working Group operated on a basis of consensus [...]. In most cases, whenever a difficulty on an issue or on a formulation arose, an informal working party was formed, consisting of participants with various opinions and proposals, who had to reach consensus *en petit comité*. Many times this procedure had good results, as delegates were willing and pushed for a workable solution. [...] It was unavoidable that in such a setting some issues could not be settled. These were issues on the 'minimum age' of the child, in other words permitting the outlawing of abortion; the freedom to choose (another) religion, which is prohibited under Islamic law; the protection of children in inter-country adoption; and, the age at which children should be permitted to take part in armed conflict.

> (Koren 1996: 169–170; see also *United Nations, Office of the High Commissioner for Human Rights* (2007))

This drafting process was unusual and in several respects historically unparalleled. It was remarkable for its dialogues, its will to find compromises, its commitment to consensus on the text in the working groups, for the huge influence from NGOs and for the close collaboration between around 50 NGOs, the UN and the governments of the concerned countries (Koren 1996: 169–170; Alston 2004: 183; Brett 2012: 244). One explanation why this broad co-work was possible was that the CRC was created at a politically very special time. The Cold War was coming to an end, making it possible for countries from the West and the East to reach an agreement (Brett 2012: 244; Alston 2004: 189). Further, also countries from the South, including Islamic states, as well as many former colonies also took part in the process in their own right (Koren 1996: 170). The *Convention of the Rights of the Child* has been seen as "both a post-cold-war and post-colonial treaty" (Grahn-Farley 2013: 290):

> The CRC's adoption had been hailed as 'a landmark at the end of the Cold War—the first international legal instrument adopted by consensus, bridging two political blocs, bridging the North and the South, bridging civil rights and freedoms with economic, social and cultural rights, bridging state accountability with the active involvement of the civil society.' (Marta Santos Pais in Brett 2012: 245)

The CRC was adopted unanimously by the UN General Assembly on 20 November 1989, and it entered into force on 2 September 1990 (CRC). Today all countries are parties to it, expect Somalia and the USA, who have only signed it (Brett 2012: 244). Further, CRC has been the most widely and rapidly ratified convention in the history of the UN (Archard 2015: 107), and "it is by far the most detailed and comprehensive (in terms of the rights recognized, as opposed to the categories of persons covered) of all of the existing international human rights instruments" (Alston 2004: 183).

The moral and legal change with the *Convention of the Rights of the Child* was not the giving of legal rights, but *what* legal rights children are now given (Koren 1996: 165). There are five guiding principles of the CRC: (1) the right not to be discriminated against, (2) the best interest of the child, (3) that state parties shall use their 'maximum extent of available resources' for the implementation of the CRC, (4) the child's right to life, and (5) the child's right to be heard in all matters concerning the child (Grahn-Farley 2013: 242–243).[4] That CRC came to include not only social and economic rights but also civil and political rights was the most important change from former international legal instruments on children (Freeman 2012: 1–7).'The right to be heard' entails not only to be an object of care and a subject with an interest in living a good life but also to be a subject with the right to have a voice and participate in decisions regarding his or her own life. Though the CRC's impact on actually bettering the lives of children is debated, most scholars hold a positive view of its legal as well as moral and practical merits and consider it an example of moral progress (Brett 2012; Grahn-Farley 2013; Ishay 2008)[5]:

> in the twenty-five years since its adoption, the CRC has exercised an extraordinarily pervasive and significant influence on the way in which law- and policy-makers think about the status of children. The CRC is the benchmark against which governments and their critics judge progress in the field of children's rights. (Archard 2015: 107)

Yet, as Archard also laconically remarks, "the worldwide systematic abuse of children's rights continues" (Archard 2015: 109; see also Dübeck 2013: 59; Ishay 2008: 303).

The story of the background and creation of the *Convention of the Rights of the Child* contains a diversity of dynamics, many of which have been seen in the former cases. Only a few will be highlighted here. A main dynamic in the creation of the CRC was *politics*. We see this dynamic at play in countless ways. Among other things did the political climate from 1979 to 1989 enable a very broad international consensual co-work, which allowed the document to be both wide in scope and afterwards widely ratified and respected. The CRC is now a globally recognised and

[4] Some scholars claim that there are only four guiding principles (Freeman 2012: 6; Koren 1996: 172; Van Buren 1995: 15). Archard says there are only three: "It is standard now to categorize the rights that are given to the child within the CRC in terms of the three P's: provision, protection, and participation" (Archard 2015: 110). Other researchers operate with only two (Koren 1996: 173).

[5] There are dissenting voices to the idea of human rights as moral progress, see, for instance, Zigon (2013) and Freeman (2012). Attempts at addressing these worries can be found in Nickel (2014, 2007: 168–178), Tumulty (2009), Bates (2014: 27–28), Ishay (2008), Hunt (2008), and Archard (2015: 107–109).

applied measuring rod on the quality of children's lives and of the treatment of them by states, institutions and parents, and many states take their lead from it when revising their child laws.

It can also be argued that 'the power of trends' is to be seen in this case. Since the 1950s 'human rights' have become legal and moral fashion, in the sense that today many people blindly believe that major problem with serious moral significance can and should be solved through the legal tool of human rights (Zigon 2013). Human rights further have, as Hunt points out, an inbuilt tendency "to cascade" (Hunt 2008: 147)—there is no natural end point to the creation of them, which makes them a powerful trend. If children and Indigenous Peoples deserve special human rights, what about transgender people and humanoid robots and so forth?

In this section we were also reminded of how the wish and attempt *to protect what is considered moral valuable* is an influential dynamic of moral change. Part of the wish to create the CRC was that the earlier international human rights instruments failed to take good enough care of the particular needs and vulnerability of children, whose lives we consider especially valuable today. A recurring dynamic in the stories in this part is *attempts to relieve suffering* of various kinds: starvation, injustice, disease, unnecessary death, rape, exploitation, orphanage, fear, abuse, participation in armed conflicts, the breaking up of families and being driven away from one's home. Further, the wish to protect world peace and democratic societies was also part of the motivation for the USA and many countries in Europe in their creation of international law such as the CRC.

In the next, concluding section of Part I, I will unfold which general account of the dynamics and structures of moral changes, I believe emerges from the eight narratives, and the hopes we can have for creating moral progress.

CHAPTER 10

# Conclusion: Army of Metaphors

> I am insisting that *any* account of historical change *must* in the end account for the alteration of individual minds. For human rights to become self-evident, ordinary people *had* to have new understandings that came from new kinds of feelings. (Hunt 2008: 34, my italics)

One of the attractions of attaining a clear conceptual overview of the dynamics and structures of moral change was the hope that such understanding could be a basic theoretical framework for empirical research into change as well as allow us to make better decisions in, for example, politics. It thus holds the hope of being a part of enabling social progress and avoid wasted resources and harm.

If our aim is to actively create moral changes, it seems the most attractive strategy to develop a theory of either the dynamic(s) *necessarily* driving moral changes or, if that is not possible, the dynamic(s) *mainly* responsible for creating moral changes.[1] Either form of theory would be a very powerful tool in the creation of future progress. Hunt gives voice to an idea like the former in the quote introducing this chapter. Appiah can be interpreted to be advancing a theory of the latter kind in the book *The Honor Code—How Moral Revolutions Happen* (2010) (Laidlaw 2011; Eriksen 2019).

[1] A preliminary way of explaining the term 'dynamic' is to say that the dynamics of a change are what can be presented as the answer to the question '*Why* did this change happen?' (or, as we shall see, a possible part of what can be so presented).



C. Eriksen, *Moral Change*,
https://doi.org/10.1007/978-3-030-61037-1_10

The attraction and popularity of 'the general explanatory theory' as a model of understanding in the humanities and the social sciences stems from its triumphs in greatly increasing our understanding in the natural sciences as well as helping us control countless aspects of the physical world, thereby diminish major evils such as starvation, diseases and premature deaths in many parts of the world. The successes of such encompassing explanatory theories that features only a small number of fundamental laws or general rules, capable of explaining a large number of diverse phenomena, make it tempting for us to aim for the same kind of understanding and control over the social world. This leads to theory-building and a search for recurring, fundamental dynamics explaining the unfolding of, for instance, moral changes and revolutions.

To put forward this kind of theory will, however, not be the road this concluding chapter travels for reasons given ahead. Instead, I will present alternative models of understanding the dynamics as well the structures of moral change, and in doing so also gesture at different ways of attaining social and moral change.[2]

## Dynamics: An Irreducible Plurality

Which general conceptualisation of the dynamics of moral change do the earlier provided eight narratives suggest? The first trait to notice is that they display a *variety* of dynamics leading to different kinds of moral change. To mention some of them, it was shown how a law-created economic incitement led to increased harm doing of orphans in Sweden, and how colonisation caused the destruction of the life conditions for the traditional Crow life, which forced a change of their fundamental moral framework and form of life. We saw how increased scientific knowledge of

[2] The term 'theory' has no unison use in academia, and it covers what seems to be several different concepts. Schiller (2016) describes the diversity of the term's meanings in anthropology. To that can be added the various uses of it in the social sciences and all of the humanities (and probably also a variety of uses in the natural sciences). What we are left with is a very complex picture. My critique and rejection in the following of a theory of moral change is therefore not directed at everything called 'a theory of moral change', but only a general explanatory theory of fundamental and recurring dynamics of moral change. I use terms like 'a general account', 'metaphors of', 'a conceptual overview', 'knowledge of', and 'a conception of' to designate some of the forms of conceptualisations I believe we can develop of moral changes. These are things often also referred to as 'a theory' in academia. But for heuristic reasons, I choose not to do so. For two different defences of the use of the term 'theory' in the humanities, see Nussbaum (2000) and Hämäläinen (2006).

the causal connections between smoking and diseases motivated the Danish politicians to pass a law on smoking and how general cultural obedience to laws created a change of smoking practice and the moral evaluation of smoking in the Danish population. The narratives showed how factors such as a changed ideal for childhood, the spread of information through newspapers and engaging art in the form of novels, poems and drawings motivated political lobbing, which eventually lead to a betterment of the working conditions of children during the industrialisation. We saw how legal battles, the media and international pressure lead to the beginning of a rebirth of justice for the native nations in Canada, and how in the Middle Ages a threat to human survival motivated the development of a new practice for dealing with human harm-doing, which sparred the lives of many men and improved the quality of life in European societies.

The work of other researcher calls attention to further dynamics, some present and others absent in the narratives provided earlier. For instance, in her work, Moody-Adams mentions the articulation of rational arguments that expose inconsistencies (as was part of what happened when the political commitment to liberal consistency led to decriminalisation of homosexuality in Denmark), to reveal falsehoods and delusions (as happened when the American politics 'separate but equal' was shown to be inequality), and address various forms of ignorance (as when doctors proved that deformities in infants were not caused by the moods of the mother) (Moody-Adams 2017: 158; my added parenthesis). Anthropologist Joel Robbins' investigations of the conversion of the Urapmin people in Papua New Guinea to a form of charismatic Christianity document how a group's wish to retain high status and religious power among other religious groups can be a strong dynamic in creating moral changes throughout their society (Robbins 2004, 2007). Appiah argues that changes in a group's honour codes were part of the dynamics leading to the abandonment of slavery, of duelling in England and foot-binding in China (Appiah 2010). Bicchieri's work focusses on social norm entrepreneurship as a tool for moral progress (Bicchieri 2017) and Sunstein's on preference changes (Sunstein 2019). In *Inventing Human Rights—a History*, Hunt focusses on the role of individuals' emotions in creating social and moral changes by describes how the very speedy acceptance of the idea of human rights for all human beings as *self-evident* can in part be explained by the spread of the reading of novels like *Clarissa: Or the History of a Young Lady* (Hunt 2008: 47).

A dynamics in human life, which a focus on the practice of law and narratives based on legal history easily ends up downplaying, because legal changes most often happens as the result of decisions, is the human capacity to act spontaneously. Wittgenstein notes: "We decide on a new language-game. We decide *spontaneously* (I should like to say) on a new language-game" (Wittgenstein 2001: Part 4, § 23). Implicit in this quote is a picture of humans as being able to start something new—to be *founders* of, for example, new fads, new practices, new ways of living. We can do so and have reasons for it, like doctors had for changing their practice of prescribing Thalidomide. But Wittgenstein here reminds us that humans also sometimes act without being forced to do so and without having any particular reason to do so.

This 'lack of grounds' for decisions can to some extent be seen in cases of moral change, which, for example happen due to 'leaps of faith' (Pleasants 2018). If we think of the Crow, then they had to make decisions at a time when their form of life, worldview and conceptual framework to a large extent were crumbling—and therefore it was not fruitful to appeal to their ordinary rationality, when deciding how to move forward. In this context, some of their judging, deciding and acting took on the form of leaps of faith:

> At a time of cultural collapse, the courageous person has, as it were, to take a risk on the framework itself. Plenty Coups had to risk inadvertently taking himself and his people down a shameful path—at a time before the framework in which shame could be evaluated was firmly established. (Lear 2008: 112)

Even though the Crow's decisions did have some grounds in a child's religious vision and the experiences the natives had had with the colonisers up to this point, the Crow's actions are also leaps of faith. History gives vindication to many of the decisions the Crow made, it seems from Lear's narrative; yet there is no doubt that the Crow took a colossal ethical risk in their choices.

Morrison states: "There is not a one-size-fits-all explanation of historical events" (Morrison 2012: 246). My conclusion is that the same is the case with moral changes. Moral changes can happen due to a variety of dynamics. One class of such dynamics is *causal dynamics* forcing a change. The example of this was the colonising powers. The traditional Crow way of life could not *not* change as a result of the colonisation.[3] Yet causal dynamics can to a stronger or lesser degree force moral changes upon us, so we can here talk of degrees of voluntary/involuntary changes. Many of the moral changes in Crow life and culture were involuntary and forced upon them, but some of them not entirely so, as the way the Crow handled and responded to the destruction of their culture also shaped the moral changes they went through.

Another class of dynamics is *non-causal dynamics*. One example of this is when humans—as individuals or as a collective—decide to make a change based on reasons. This may lead to *intended* moral changes, as the development of the compensations system instead of feuds. But humans acting out of reasons may also lead to *unintended* moral changes, like *a side-effect* to something they do—as the deterioration of living conditions for orphaned children in the 'Angel maker'-case or some of the betterments of the living conditions for homosexuals in Denmark can remind us.

Furthermore, the reasons that can motivate humans to create a moral change are far from unison in nature, but can be 'economic gain', 'to attain justice', 'the wish to survive', 'to follow a legal fashion', 'to reduce suffering', 'to live up to an ideal', 'to avoid bad publicity', 'greed', 'to further health', 'the wish to be consistent', 'to hold on to high religious status and power' or 'to follow the Gods' visions', to name a few.

Lastly, moral changes may also happen due to *a mixture* of causal forces and non-causal dynamics. This happens when we try to adapt our form of life to climate changes or to deadly, global pandemics. There is thus no unique group of dynamics that can be singled out as 'the *moral* dynamics', by which all moral changes can be properly explained. Moral change happens for the same reasons and causes as all other kinds of historical changes do.

Moreover, I want to argue that the concept of the drives of moral change is not only pluralistic, it is *irreducibly* pluralistic. By that I mean that there is not one recurring dynamic (or group of dynamics), which is necessary for any moral change to happen and which has the role as the fundamental change creating factor—that which ultimately explains why any moral change happens.

[3] The narratives did not display many examples of moral change being causally forced, but, for instance, also changes in nature can force a change in our concepts and practices (see, e.g. Wittgenstein 2009: §§ 142, 480–486, 2016: §§ 513–619).

One reason why I want to conclude this is that the narratives above all *made sense*, despite the fact that there were no recurring explanatory dynamics to be found in them. It might be historically rare that a person is driven purely by altruistic motives to change her society. It might also be rare that moral change in a practice is created by chance, as the unintended side effect of other changes made for economic reasons. But it is not a priori impossible that this could happen (like it is impossible that I stumble upon a round square on my evening walk along the river Cam). This would not have been the case if the concept of a dynamic capable of creating a moral change was reducible to one or a few main dynamics.

Another way of substantiating this point is to borrow a conceptual tool from Wittgenstein's discussions in the philosophy of language, namely 'family-resemblance-concept' (Wittgenstein 2009: §§ 66–69). A family-resemblance concept is a word with a family of uses, which does not have one common trait, but displays a complicated pattern consisting of criss-crossing similarities and differences—like the criss-crossing of similarities and differences we see in the physical appearance of members in a large kin-group (they do not all have 'the same kind of nose', but some do, they do not all have read hair, freckles and blue eyes, but many do, almost all of them are big-boned, but then there is 'skinny aunt Magda', etc.).

I believe we should follow Winch and see 'explanation' as a family resemblance concept and say that humans have developed several different 'explanation-language-games' (Winch 2008: 15–17, 67–88). Some forms of explanation language-games are mainly found in the natural sciences, some in the social sciences, some still in religious practices and so forth, and most of them in some form in our everyday life. In the natural sciences, we explain the unfolding of changes in the phenomena we investigate purely with references to various form of causes, but never reasons. The electron jumps between different energy states in the atom, not because it has a reason to do so, like it was bored or needed the exercise, but because energy was added to the system, and then it was forced to jump. In the social sciences, like in psychology, we can explain changes with references to both causes and reasons/motives. The man killed his wife, because she had been deceiving him (reason), or, the man killed his wife, because he had a brain tumour that made him act irrationally (cause). In religious practices, we also operate with both causes and reasons, like he did it because he was obsessed by an evil spirit/devil (cause), or he did it because the Gods send him a vision or told him to do so in the form of thundering voice from the sky (reason). There is a categorical difference between explaining human behaviour in terms of causal dynamics, such as mutations in the human genome, and explaining it in terms of motivational dynamics, such as a political motivation to do something (Wittgenstein 2009: § 325, II: 114–115, 2016: § 474). Both can be explanations of why some event happens, and both can be wrong, right or misplaced concerning a given situation. But they are two different forms of explanation belonging to different language-games with each having their aims, rules, conditions and criteria.

Which explanation-language-game it is illuminating and justifiable to play, when seeking to understand why a particular moral change happened, depends on the context and kind of phenomenon we are investigating. All explanation-language-games have conditions and criteria for when it is meaningful or legitimate to play them and failing to comply with these will result in distorting or pseudo explanations of the phenomenon in question, and then what is provided is not recognisable as an explanation of the phenomenon in question (Wittgenstein 1993a; Orsi 2016: 62–65). If I were to insist that, for instance, all the changes in fine dining and the culinary world evolve only because of struggles between chefs to win fame and recognition, I seem to oversimplify and thus distort the phenomena I am interested in by missing they are also driven and motivated by playfulness and experimental curiosity, by the wish to create joy and elation in their restaurant guests, to perfect or develop the culinary tradition they spring from, to bread cultural understanding and tolerance, to incarnate beauty, to pioneer new ways of creating food, new understandings of what food is or new ways of dealing with issues such as animal welfare, health and sustainability. And if I want to understand why my six-year-old transformed from glad to sulky one day, it would be out of place as my first reaction was to take her to a neurologist and ask to get her brain scanned to see if a tumour affected her mood, rather than sitting down and asking her if anything was bothering her. Conversely, if she started to have regular fits, falling unconscious to the floor with her whole body shaking violently, it would be odd to ask her to explain why she was having these fits, instead of taking her to see a doctor.

One of the dangers we face, in adopting the natural scientific model of an explanatory theory, when seeking to understand moral changes on a general level, is to assume that one dynamics is the primary or one of these explanation-language-games is the most fundamental—that when all comes to all, it *must* be, for example, individual psychology, economic interest or evolutionary benefits that drives all or most moral changes. The danger here is to present an oversimplifying, distorted or false image of the human life and life world. Based on the conceptual investigation of this book, I believe we are searching in vain, if searching for such a dynamic. Because the eight narratives above all displayed a row of different and no universally recurring dynamics and because all narratives still made sense as possible scenarios of moral changes (no matter what the factual truth-value of the narratives are), I believe it should be concluded that there are no particular dynamics *necessary* for moral change, and further, that the concept of 'a dynamic of moral change' encompasses an *irreducible plurality* of different dynamics.

So far, my focus has been on which kind of dynamics may create moral change. But the eight narratives also indicate that a focus on particular dynamics hides other aspects, which are equally important to get into view, when we seek to understand moral change; something I will unfold in the next sections, where I look into the structures of moral changes.

## Structures: Weaves, Dawns and Meteor Strikes

Earlier I argued that there are no specific dynamic(s) necessary for moral changes, which universally explain how they happen, like the chemical properties of the molecule H2O can explain the behaviour of all the phenomenologically very different phenomena of water, ice, steam and snow. This does not rule out that a *particular* change can be explained with reference to one or several dynamics. However, stories about how dynamics *x*, *y* and *z* lead to change *q*—that is, picturing dynamics as 'distinct transformers', as singular, isolatable threads in the weave of life—can make us miss that this picture, though apt in some cases, does not capture the structure and unfolding of *all* moral changes. This image can therefore mislead us in regard as to how to understand and create some forms of change. In this section I will unfold alternative pictures to the 'distinct dynamics-picture', which will give more prominence to the role of *context*.

As a way of getting started, Wittgenstein has this insult to offer to historians and social scientists: "Who knows the laws according to which society unfolds? I am sure even the cleverest has no idea" (Wittgenstein 2006: 69). And later he adds another: "E.g. nothing [is] more stupid than the chatter about cause & effect in history books: nothing more wrong-headed, more half-baked" (Wittgenstein 2006: 71).

In the earlier given eight narratives, it did in many cases make sense and was historically justifiable to point to some dynamics as playing a more prominent transformative role than others. The metaphor of 'a meteor stroke'—that is, the violent breakthrough of an alien, external and distinct factor causing a devastating change in the existing environment—is a useful image for understanding how and why the traditional Crow way of life initially started to change. We have further seen changes unfold in both 'top-down' (e.g. in the case of the first de-moralising of homosexuality in Denmark) and 'bottom-up'-manners (e.g. the expansion of the equal legal rights of homosexuals in Denmark). In other words, talk of 'cause and effect' in books of history and in the social sciences is hardly always 'stupid chatter'.

However, history and life do seem to contain episodes, which challenges the universal usefulness of understanding moral changes in human forms of life through the images of 'cause and effect' or 'distinct dynamics'. If we return to the cases of the change of labour laws for children and the passing of the Convention for the Rights of the Child, this starts to show. It is not wrong to say that these changes happened due to, for instance, changes in the *concept* of the child, changes in the *ideals* for childhood, changes in the *economy*, the attainment of new *scientific knowledge* of children, changes in the internal and external *power* and *political structures* of societies. But to some extent, the dynamics leading to the passing of these laws and what many see as a betterment of the life conditions of children seem to have a 'chicken-and-egg'-character, making it tricky—and perhaps even impossible—to state what initially led to what. Did our ideals for and understanding of children change because of new insights gained from scientific research into child psychology, which documented, say, the harmfulness of physical and humiliating punishments, or did we only pursue these scientific investigations because our ideals for and conceptions with respect to childhood had already changed, thereby making such research a meaningful option? It is possible that there isn't an 'either/or-answer' to give in this and in similar cases, because the dynamics were intertwined and influencing each other, and they merged in a feedback loop. For that reason, we cannot in such cases "disentangle the personal, social, economic, and cultural factors", as Bicchieri suggests we do (Bicchieri 2017: 1). In some cases, it is a complicated *weave* of interrelated, mutually affecting and merging factors that is creating a change. These types of developments can be termed *holistic*.

Another example of such holistic development on an individual level can be found in Pleasant's recounting of going from having absorbed what he saw as his society's 'homophobic, racist and sexist beliefs' during the time he grew up to abandoning them as a grown up:

> I myself cannot identify any particular experiential or cognitive events that made me, or enabled me to, realise that the racist, sexist, etc. beliefs and attitudes that I harboured, and the practices, institutions and way of life that they supported, were morally deleterious. Not could I, with any precision, specify the time at which this realization occurred; it was gradual and processual shift, clearly only in retrospect. (Pleasants 2018: 4)

Rather than the metaphor of a meteor, here the metaphor of *dawn* seems helpful in understanding the structure of how holistic changes unfold. When the sun rises and morning comes, the "light dawns gradually" (Wittgenstein 2016: § 141), unlike when we switch on a light bulb in a dark room. At dawn, light spreads like a fog. This metaphor may help us look at moral change as something not always happening because of distinguishable, singular acts, events or forces, but as sometimes evolving in a fluid and cohesive manner. The change Pleasants underwent happened to him. Not by his own active workings, nor by the direct workings of somebody else. The moral tide of his culture changed, and he changed with it.

Large-scale moral evolutions in societies and forms of life often seem to be holistic in structure. To use another enigmatic quote by Wittgenstein, we can say of them: "This, too, admits of being '*explained*' and not explained" (Wittgenstein 1993a: 123). They admit of being "*explained*" because we can often point to certain dynamics being important factors in creating the change. And they do *not* admit of being explained either because of, for example, a 'chicken-and-egg-'/'feedback-loop'-effect of the dynamics or because the context was equally needed to create the change. In some cases, it can thus be the situation *as a whole*, which is creating the change, and here it does not make sense to isolate singular dynamics as the responsible transformers. Social science and legal history taught us that passing a law was a very effective way of creating a desired moral change in Denmark anno 2007. However, it would not be so in all societies. It was so in the context of a particular society in a particular historical period. That is why the knowledge we gain of main dynamics in one situation cannot necessarily be transposed to other situations, allowing us to create changes in them; something which both the 'distinct dynamics of change' and the 'general explanatory theory' models make it tempting to assume, as they leave the potential role of context out of the picture.

The theme of 'explained and not explained' leads us to another aspect of the structure of moral change, which my focus on 'the dynamics of moral change' has not brought clearly out so far. A salient trait of the later Wittgenstein's work is the attempt to counter over-rationalistic conceptions of human life, such as the all-too-human urge to seek explanations and justifications for everything. It is a tendency he criticises in no uncertain terms: "Our mistake is to look for an explanation where we ought to regard the facts as 'proto-phenomena'" (Wittgenstein 2009: § 654). Or as he puts it elsewhere, "Our disease is one of wanting to explain" (Wittgenstein 2001: Part 6: 31). I believe that countering a rationalistic image as a global approach to human life is also relevant when it comes to understanding moral change:

> You must bear in mind that the language-game is so to say something unpredictable. I mean: it is not based on grounds. It is not reasonable (or unreasonable). It is there—like our life. (Wittgenstein 2016: § 559)

That the language-games—and our life—"is here", beyond reasonable and unreasonable, and "so to say is something unpredictable", entails that it does not always make sense to look at the evolution of human forms of life as something which can, or should, be explained.[4] The question "Why did this moral change happen?", craving for causes or reasons explaining the change, can be misplaced. Sometimes we are "*wrongly* expecting an explanation" (Wittgenstein 2004: § 314, my italics). We do so not because the dynamics are hidden from us, and not because the matter is too complicated to sort out, but because in some cases an explanation is *uncalled* for (as in the first remark quoted below)—and in others it *lacks sense* (as in the example of the second remark cited next):

> I see a picture; it represents an old man walking up a steep path leaning on a stick.—How? Might it not have looked just the same if he had been sliding downhill in that position? Perhaps a Martian would describe the picture so. I don't need to explain why *we* don't describe it so. (Wittgenstein 2009: § 139, boxed remark b)

[4] See, for example, Hopf (2018) for similar considerations. To try to counter *over*-rationalistic understandings of human life, and, for example, carve out a space for the spontaneous, or the religious, or the instinctive, is not, of course, to argue for an irrational understandings of human life or to be 'against science' or anything if this sort.

> What does man think for? What is it good for? [...] Does man think, then, because he has found that thinking pays?—Because he thinks it advantageous to think? (Does he bring his children up because he has found it pays?) (Ibid: § 466, 467)

Wittgenstein's string of questions in the latter quote leads his reader "from unobvious nonsense to obvious nonsense" (Ibid: § 464). We can explain particular instances of thinking as something that is undertaken because it has proved advantageous to do so in similar instances—such as, when we have learned to 'think before speaking, when angry' (see also Ibid: § 469–470). It would, however, be an absurd over-rationalisation to explain *all* forms of thinking this way, as most of the time humans think exactly in the same way as they breathe—as part of their spontaneous existence as the kind of creatures they are. There is nothing more fundamental or illuminating to offer as an explanation of it—our explanations-spade has reach bedrock. An image for these forms of moral evolutions could therefore be the blind, organic growth and decay of a forest or colonies of fungi. We can at times have a need to offer explanations as to how and why they evolve, but there is less temptation to do so generally.

In cases were explanation is uncalled for or lacks sense, Wittgenstein's advice is that the understanding we seek of these fundamental aspects of life can be gained through description and reminders: "Here one can only *describe* and say: this is what human life is like" (Wittgenstein 1993a: 121). A refined skill to do so can be found among great poets, authors of novels and moral anthropologists, who are all able to increase our understanding of 'what human life is like' without trying to tame and control it through analytical schemes and explanatory theories.

To sum the conclusions of the last sub-sections up: the general account of moral change, I have developed, has three main characteristics. Firstly, the claim that moral changes do not have a set of recurring characteristics explaining why they happen, and that the dynamics capable of leading to them are *irreducibly pluralistic*. Secondly, it allows for *holistic* developments, and lastly, the view that some moral development in and of human forms of life unfolds *spontaneously* and *organically*, in ways 'beyond justified and unjustified, beyond explainable or unexplainable' (a theme I return to in Part II). In the next section, I will look at the consequences that this understanding of moral change has for the hope of change creation.

## The Hope of Change Creation

As mentioned earlier, if we could locate the dynamics either necessary or generally responsible for moral changes, then we would have a powerful tool for creating future transformations of harmful beliefs, traditions and institutions—we would know which handles to turn (see, e.g. Appiah 2010: xvii, 170–172). However, the conception of moral change developed here offers strong reservations about this hope.

Firstly, it does so by displaying a plurality of different dynamics, where none of them is assigned the role as the fundamental and recurring change-crating dynamic(s). If our concept of a dynamic capable of leading to a change is irreducibly pluralistic in this way (i.e. if explanation is a family resemblance concept), then we have prima facie reason to be sceptical towards any theory presenting us with universal or very general handles to turn in order to create moral changes in the human life world.[5] Secondly, it also does so by entailing the possibility of holistic developments; that some changes happen on the background of the situation as a whole and not only because of certain main drivers. This means that even if it is possible to establish as a fact that a type of change in the past was driven by certain main dynamics, we nevertheless may still not be able to induce the same change in another society by turning these same handles, if the changes in question were holistic changes. Thirdly, the conception is also discouraging by pointing to the human capacity to act spontaneously, which in principle makes parts of our future inherently open and unpredictable. Moody-Adams claims that "once we understand the complex nature and complicated sources of moral progress, we will appreciate why we cannot construct a plausible action guiding theory of moral progress" (Moody-Adams 2017: 153). All of the above supports this conclusion and speaks against any high hopes of finding the kind of knowledge of the past, which translates into a general explanatory theory enabling us to control the future development of human life. Is the consequence of this conception that we can attain no forms of knowledge of moral change and that no models are able to guide us in change creation? I believe both worries are unwarranted, and I will address them both in the following.

[5] If theories of this kind are presenting a false, oversimplified or in other ways distorted image of human life then this is something that would need to be shown from case to case and cannot be proven 'once and for all' (Wittgenstein 2016: § 37; Eriksen 2019).

A worry, which an irreducibly pluralistic and partly holistic and organic conception of moral change can raise, is that it entails 'a Heracleitean morass'.[6] A Heracleitean morass is the view that it is never possible in any justifiable or meaningful way to state what lead to what, because everything is in flux, all dynamics and events melt into each other, and all that happens is influenced by and influencing everything else. This morass means that we can never establish any valid general knowledge about any dynamics of change. All we can claim is that 'everything changes', and 'life is complicated'. Any hope of learning from the past in order to improve our future must therefore be abandoned.[7] The radical conclusion that follows from the image of such a morass it is not one I believe, should be drawn based on the investigations of this book.

The aim of this book is to give a philosophical understanding of moral change. In this part, this aim is sought by a row of reminders in the form of the eight narratives of historical changes and by providing a synoptic presentation of 'the space of possibilities' for how moral change can unfold. A philosophical investigation cannot establish how any type of moral change *actually* unfolds, or how they most *generally* unfold, if they do so, as the latter are empirical questions, which lie outside the prominence of philosophy. The understanding worked out here provides a better basic conceptual frame and basis for future empirical investigations and active change creation than theories, which insist on certain dynamics as the fundamental drives of all moral change, because the latter blinds us (too much) to the complexity of moral change.

A rejection of a general explanatory theory of moral change as such does not, however, preclude the attainment of historical, anthropological, sociological, economic or psychological knowledge of moral changes. It is possible that there are regularities in dynamics of moral changes to be found through various forms of empirical research into much more specified areas of life and regarding much more specified questions and problems, compared to an investigation into moral change as such. This could, for example, be the case with 'child development' or 'corruption of democratic practices' and countless other demarcated areas and problems of the human lifeworld. Such knowledge could be part of what successfully

[6] The word is borrowed from Burian (2001: 399), but it has a different meaning in his article.

[7] See Pitt (2001: 378) for a similar line of reasoning in the philosophy of science.

guides the development of educational institutions, where children thrive and political institutions where less corruption is bred. The Facebook-Cambridge Analytica data scandal (where predictions and psychological profiles based on data about 50 million Facebook users' past "clicking-habits" were utilised to target some users with tailored political slogans and images, which is assumed to have manipulated their future votes and the outcome of the American presidential election in 2016) is one example showing that and how we can use knowledge of the past to shape the future. The fact that some governments so far have been able to avoid a too violent spread of the coronavirus also supports the belief that humans can control the developments of some changes in our societies based on area-and problem-specific general knowledge of the past.

The reason why we need the attainment of knowledge to be area and problem *specific* is that this is what supply us with criteria and measuring rods for what it is *relevant* to investigate, for what is essential, fundamental or accidental, and for which concepts, theories and methods are helpful to employ in the investigation. It is possible that we can develop, for instance, a good systematic typology of the driving mechanisms of the moral developments of children. This could be helpful for educational purposes for parents, pedagogues, teachers, psychologists and child doctors. It could also be put to good use in designing toys, teaching materials for schools and countless other things. Such a systematic typology will, of course, need revisions from time to time, and most likely it will sooner or later be revolutionised, and a new typology developed (see, e.g. Kuhn 1970; Baker 2019). But nonetheless, it can be an aid in creating social and moral progress in a specific area of life. What we cannot do is to develop such a systematic typology of the driving mechanisms of all possible forms of moral change as such, because here nothing is guiding the relevance of our categorisations and investigation methods.

Besides the attainment of area-specific and problem-guided knowledge, there are also models of understanding which may direct the creation of future progress and help us deal with changes (other than the general explanatory theory). One such approach could take its lead from Hämäläinen's work. In her article, Hämäläinen offers three metaphors as a help for understanding moral change (Hämäläinen 2017). To take a lead from this approach in the active creation of social and moral changes could be to build 'a mobile army of metaphors', to borrow a classic poetic-aggressive expression from Nietzsche. A mobile army of metaphors would be an open collection of different metaphors for understanding the dynamics and structures of change.

Metaphors and images for the dynamics and structures of moral change used in this book were, for example, 'the meteor', 'the dawn', 'the hen and the egg', 'a rebirth', 'a weave of threads', 'a shift of tide', 'feedback loops' and 'a leap of faith'. Other researchers have used 'the tipping-point' (a small internal shift in the balance of factors in a system leading to a significant change, like Rosa Park's refusal to give up her bus seat, NY police raiding of the Stonewall Inn and, perhaps, the killing of George Floyd), 'the bargaining table' (where moral change happens as the result of active agents, like the political dialogue and give and take-process leading to the CRC), 'drips becoming a flood' (when many minor changes adds up to a moral revolution), and Adams Smith's 'invisible hand' (where unintended social benefits arise from the actions of a groups of purely self-interested individuals) (see, e.g. Hämäläinen 2017; Sunstein 2019; Baker 2019).

A metaphor is not a theory, and it does not claim to exhaustively explain or depict reality 1:1. A metaphor offers us *a way of seeing* a situation, and as such it can also suggest ways of *handling* it. Benefits of this approach is that a collection of metaphors, I believe, to a lesser degree than one general explanatory theory make us confuse the model of reality and reality like we do when we insist that, ultimately, all moral change *must* be explained by, for instance, changes in individuals' feelings, brain chemistry, what helps group survival, a struggle for power, economic interest, or whichever dynamic is currently the intellectual fashion to summon as the ultimate driving mechanism of human life.

Further, a metaphor, like a poem, contains a poetic surplus of meaning, which cannot be fully spelled out or exhausted, even if we can explain its meaning(s). To develop an army of a metaphors of change can therefore be an important wellspring of creativity that opens our imagination and is as such an important supplement to a clear conceptual understanding, systematic topologies of types of dynamics, historical insight and the relevant empirical knowledge, when we face a need for creating changes in our life and society. No matter which tool we reach for in the tool-box, an appreciation of each particular case and context is crucial for the successful creation of social and moral change, and that is something we can never exhaustively codify, but only cultivate.

CHAPTER 11

# Interlude: The Normative Challenges of Moral Change

I have now offered a general philosophical account of the unfolding of moral change. However, I still need to address the troubling moral and philosophical worries mentioned in the Introduction that arise from moral change. After reading the eight narratives, a sceptical interlocutor could respond: Very well, you have described how some moral changes unfold and which dynamics may create them. But how do these descriptions, reminders and narratives answer our ethical worries, like how any of us can be ethically *justified* in acting, in deciding, in evaluating, and in judging not only related to the practices of former times, but to our practices and institutions today, when our moral ideals, values and criteria are in flux? How can we *trust* our current moral values, ideas and ideals when the old ones turned out to be ethically untrustworthy, misleading us to do bad and not good? What is the *objective* mark of ethical trustworthiness?

> If principles cannot claim to be constitutively independent from the contingent morass that feeds our ethical sensitivity, *where can resistance to our acting as usual spring from?* [...] *what if we simply care about the wrong things?* (Delacroix forthcoming: 2, 8, my italics)

If moral change is accepted, then the ethical legitimacy and trustworthiness of our moral tools and the possibility of ethical critique seem to crumble in our hands, while we try to apply them—and not only to what is in 'the historical distance' (Moody-Adams 1999: 8; 2002: 61), but also


C. Eriksen, *Moral Change*,
https://doi.org/10.1007/978-3-030-61037-1_11

to what is in our current present. Yet, at the same time life constantly raises ethical demands to judge, decide and act in order for us *not* to fail morally; demands we face both as individuals and as a society. Our predicament is this: It seems we cannot be ethically justified in moving, yet we are ethically called on to move. We are caught in a Gordian knot. Just describing and reminding us of how moral changes unfold does not answer these deeper and more fundamental philosophical and ethical questions. It only raises the challenge.

PART II

# The Normativity of Moral Change

> The idea of moral progress is a necessary presupposition of action for beings like us. We must believe that moral progress is possible and that it might have been realized in human experience, if we are to be confident that continued human action can have any morally constructive point. (Moody-Adams 2017: 153)

If moral change is accepted as a fact about life, this seems to challenge us in several ways, one of them is as a threat to our sense of being able to judge, decide, and act in ethically legitimate ways. Having hope and the courage to act as individuals and as a society is paramount for democracy and flourishing lives.

In this part of the book I investigate a range of challenges to moral normativity with the further aim of developing a conception of ethics I term 'contextual ethics'. The challenges all have their root in experiences of moral change, conflict, disorientation, failure and doubt. Some of the latter I refer to as 'sceptical doubts', which are general philosophical doubts, others I term 'moral doubts', which are doubts that concern and arise in a particular situation and context.

In *Philosophical Investigations* Wittgenstein writes that it does not contain one straightforward moving investigation, but sketches of a landscape seen from different angles, drawn while criss-crossing the terrain. A similar form of 'back and forth moving' investigation will unfold below, where each section deals with one aspect of the normativity of moral change, but the result is not necessarily something the next section is building on.

Sometimes the same aspect is approached again in a later section from a different angle. This approach is due to many of these investigated issues being intertwined, and further, due to the impossibility of 'saying it all at once'. For instance, discussions of the possibility and nature of radical moral changes relate to discussions of the possibility and nature of moral progress because they both involve concepts like 'evaluation', 'criteria of comparison', and 'measuring rods'. For that reason, discussions of moral evaluation appear in several of the sections. Further, as mentioned in the preface, when elaborating on what I call 'the immanent' aspects of the ethical, I will inevitably seem to neglect or betray the transcending and open aspects of the ethical, and vice versa. I therefore hope the reader will have patience with the text.

The investigation is further conducted in dialogue with ideas found in the work of philosophers like Wittgenstein, Løgstrup, Cavell, Nussbaum, Posner, Jaeggi, Rorty, Lear, and Moody-Adams, many of which have contemplated the nature of moral change.[1] In the following, we see how agreements and disagreements between thinkers shift when the topic shifts. For instance, Rorty and Posner are in fair agreement on rejecting what they term 'moral objectivism, realism and rationalism', yet they disagree on the nature and possibility of trans-historical and trans-cultural moral evaluation (Rorty 2007: 918, 921; Moody-Adams 2017: 168). However, the views of these philosophers are not discussed in depth and in their own merit. What I have attempted in the sections below is to capture possible and meaningful philosophical views on the topic of normativity in moral change; views which exist in similar forms throughout the history of philosophy as well as in the current debates on the topic.

The criterion of choice for the thinkers used in the dialogue is that they all hold philosophical positions in the middle of a meta-ethical scale ranging from moral nihilism to dogmatic moral foundationalism. All agree that forms of legitimate inter-subjective ethical evaluation, judging, and acting are possible and further, that humans do not have 'a neutral, Archimedean

[1] The odd one out in this company seems to be Wittgenstein. But Cavell, Jaeggi, Rorty, and Lear are all influenced by his thinking, and in the later years it has been shown that Wittgenstein's writings did contain what can be called 'moral philosophy'. However, my use of Wittgenstein's work in this part of the book, as also was the case in Part I, will in many cases amount to a transposing of his thinking (on topics like rule-following and the role of human attunement and nature in language-games) to topics in moral philosophy. References to his work are therefore generally not to places where Wittgenstein claim, what I write in the text, but to where I found the inspiration to claim what I claim.

standpoint' from where we can morally evaluate or justify judgements, beliefs, ideals, practices, and forms of life. But from that point on they differ. According to Delacroix one central challenge for positions in this middle field, and thus also for the contextual ethics, which this book seeks to develop, is

> accounting for the possibility of moral progress [...] If one rejects any metaphysics capable of yielding an Archimedean reference point that is safely removed from the mess one seeks to build on, how does one ascertain that progress [...] is indeed being achieved? (Delacroix forthcoming: 7)

On the same ground Nussbaum raises the broader question on the sources of moral normativity as such: When we reject the Archimedean point and a metaphysical foundationalism then 'how do we justify our moral claims? Where does the normativity of ethical norms come from?' (Nussbaum 1998: 1789). These are central questions discussed below as part of the investigation of the normativity of moral change.

CHAPTER 12

# Moral Conflict

> But what men consider reasonable or unreasonable alters. At certain periods men find reasonable what at other periods they found unreasonable. And vice versa. But is there no objective character here? (Wittgenstein 2016: § 336)

When looking back in time—or looking out horizontally to other societies and other cultures—there seems to be striking disagreements and conflicts on moral issues, like whether slavery is admissible or not, whether men and women should have equal rights and whether abortion and infanticide should be legal or not. Posner argues that when we face moral disagreements and conflicts either internally in a society, like 'hard cases' in law, or between societies, like the moral permissibility of using children as soldiers, we have no moral universals to appeal to that are of any use to us:

> There is no common ground to appeal to in arbitrating among competing moralities. [...] [it is a] brute fact that there is no consensus on any moral principles from which answers to contested moral questions might actually be derived. (Posner 1998a: 1651, 1657)

Posner's answer to the question in the aforementioned Wittgenstein quote is thus that there is no objective criterion or common ground in the form of substantial trans-historical or -cultural standards of morality. He, therefore, concludes that there can be no profitable reasoning over moral ends



C. Eriksen, *Moral Change*,
https://doi.org/10.1007/978-3-030-61037-1_12

(Posner 1998b: 1803).[1] The issue of slavery was resolved by war, not by the use of reason and argument. According to Posner, moral disagreement is thus rationally insoluble in the sense that there are no good *moral* reasons to offer 'the other party' in such a debate. However, moral disagreements and conflicts can be resolved by other means, like appeals to emotions, to scientific knowledge or instrumental considerations (Posner 1998a: 1674–1690, b: 1799). Posner's point is that when morality changes, this is never due to good moral reasons, and it is never morally justified.

Moral changes do seem to be able to be brought about by other means that appeal to moral reasons, like when the general public was moved by sentimental art to demand regulation on child labour ('*So your chimneys I sweep & in soot I sleep*'). Nonetheless Posner's view seems too extreme. For one, his picture of what a common ground can be—a standard or principles we can attain universal consensus on—seems too narrow. Why should the common ground between us have to be that—a principle? And why would a common ground be something we need to be able to attain universal *consensus* on? It seems possible people could have what in fact was a common ground and still—opaque as humans often are to ourselves—manage not to reach consensus on this. Furthermore, history does seem to offer us examples of people disagreeing morally, yet after a dialogue reaching meaningful agreement on the basis of the giving of reasons. During the creation of *The Convention of the Rights of the Child*, people from many different cultures with different moral conceptions and religious beliefs from all over the globe were debating an issue exhibiting profound moral disagreement, namely what legal rights a child should have universally. Yet, despite the many differences and disagreements, an agreement was reached, and it was reached through a ten-year dialogical and political process, which does not seem adequately reduced to only being 'instrumental considerations and emotional appeals'. During the creation of the CRC, it was debated which person's right to life 'counts the most' in relation to abortion, the mother's or the unborn child/potential child's. But it was not debated whether human life is worthy of protection. The participants in the CRC process all agreed on the

[1] Posner thinks that there does exist moral universals, which may be common to all societies, like 'murder is wrong' and a few rudimentary principles of social cooperation, such as 'Don't lie all the time', and 'Don't break promises without any reason' (Posner 1998a: 1640). They are just not potent when it comes to solving moral conflicts.

particular vulnerability of children, and they all believed that adults have an obligation to take care of this particular vulnerability. These were common moral grounds in the discussions, which allowed for the giving of moral reasons across religious, national and cultural divides. It does not seem necessary to translate these agreements into 'a standard or principle with universal consent' for these beliefs to have the role of common moral ground in the discussions.

When Posner claims that there is not enough common moral ground between different moralities to reach an agreement based on the giving of moral reasons, considerations and justifications, he seems to be wrong. There does seem to be examples, like this process of passing a piece of international law in the UN, which displays exactly this (which is not the same as to claim that no other kinds of argument and persuasive tools were used and were 'effective' in this process too, like political, legal and economic arguments). I believe it can be inferred that either Posner's 'thin' moral universals can in fact yield enough common ground for the giving of trans-cultural moral reasons, or we have more useful common moral ground between us than Posner acknowledges. The latter is the idea I will pursue. How this common ground is to be understood is not a simple matter, and I will return to the issue several times in this part of the book. What we see in the CRC case is in several respects not something adequately described as '*a* common ground', but something calling for more complicated pictures and metaphors. One such useful metaphor is transposed from Wittgenstein's work into moral philosophy by Hämäläinen:

> It can be helpful to think of morality in terms of Wittgenstein's metaphor of the fibers of a thread. What keeps a thread together and what makes it strong is not any single fiber that runs through it all the way, but rather the multitude of shorter fibers which are intertwined. When a single fiber ends it does not threaten the strength and resilience of the thread, because innumerable other fibers are there to keep it together. (Hämäläinen 2017: 63)

We do not need 'one single fiber' in the form of, for example, 'a universal principle' running through all the diverse phenomena we call 'morality' in order to find useful overlaps allowing us to communicate on moral matters, even when one thread ends and we find ourselves in disagreement over a certain issue. The historical research into the CRC process displays a fascinating picture of a complicated, multi-dimensional pattern of moral agreement and disagreement, ethical similarities and differences crisscrossing between various nations and cultures. Nations, which strongly disagree on some issues, could agree on others because they, for instance, share certain religious beliefs. Likewise, nations with religions with a history of violent clashes could reach agreement on some issues because they share, for example, a cultural tradition and an economic need for letting children participate in work from a young age.

The CRC case also point to what can be argued to be common ground between humans, namely, that the speaking of a language is common to humans across time and cultures. Not only do all humans speak languages, they speak languages, which to a high degree translate into each other. What a British Gentleman called 'nature' 200 years ago, may not overlap 100% with what a Swede today calls 'nature'. However, we translate the two words with each other, because there is enough overlap in the use of these two sounds to make a translation—and thus to some extent a mutual conversation on the topic—possible (Rorty 1989: 92, 1999: 62; Nussbaum 2001b, 2002; Moody-Adams 1999: 170–174, 2002: 7).[2] We can translate and understand *Antigone* as a tragedy about sorrow and a conflict between law and morality, something many of us know all too well, even if our religious beliefs, traditions, legal and political systems are very different from Antigone's society.

> Put otherwise, we should not call anything they do 'sacrificing', 'atoning', 'placating', etc. unless we understand how what they do could count as (grammatically be) sacrificing, atoning, placating, etc. (Cavell 1999: 111)

When thinkers like Wittgenstein, Rorty and Nussbaum explain how humans across time and cultures have overlapping vocabularies, for example, for expressing moral concerns and discussing moral matters, they all point to something that can be called 'the human form of life' or 'human nature'.

> It is in their language that human beings agree. This is agreement not in opinions, but rather in form of life. It is not only agreement in definitions, but also (odd as it may sound) agreement in judgements that is required for communication by means of language. (Wittgenstein 2009: §§ 241–242)

[2] Obviously, some words have several different uses. We can stand on a riverbank, yet that is not the place we ordinarily go to deposit our money.

The possibility of having a shared language and of translating foreign languages rests on such human attunement. Attunement shows, for example, overlaps in basic responses, needs, vulnerabilities and priorities (Rorty 1999: 62; Nussbaum 2001b: 72–76). Some moral philosophers have attempted to spell out and systematise what this common human form of life more specifically entails. Nussbaum have done so by isolating spheres "of human experience that figures in more or less any human life, and in which more or less any human being will have to make some choices rather than others, and act in some way rather than some other" (Nussbaum 2002: 245). On this background she has generated a list of central features of this common humanity, which are 'mortality', 'the body', 'pleasure and pain', 'cognitive capability', 'practical reason', 'early infant development', 'affiliation' and 'humour' (Nussbaum 2002: 263–265). This list underlines that it, and any other list or description of the common in human life, is not depicting something 'morally neutral', 'primitive given' or 'brute facts entirely neutral and free of cultural shaping' (Nussbaum 2002: 260, 263, 265). Human nature does not supply us with 'an Archimedean standpoint'. There are several reasons for this.

One is that our values and concepts are not caused by or 'read of from nature', and the meaning of them cannot be reduced to nature (Wittgenstein 2009: §§ 138–242; Nussbaum 2001b: 74, 2002: 261, 2011: 28). Any empirical fact—be it a fact about common biological or psychological needs, about genes or about brain chemistry and so forth—can be the basis for a number of different language games (Williams 1999: 158; Jaeggi 2018). Even if all humans at all times display, for example, instinctive, natural ways of reacting to pain (crying, caring, avoiding), and even if language games with the word pain is built and dependent on this pre-linguistic, universal pattern of behaviour in human life (Wittgenstein 2004: §§ 540–541, 545, 2009: § 142), then this fact still does not justify or exhaustively explain any pain-language game we have. We could have developed other concepts and practices, than we did, based on the same facts of nature, because such facts are normatively underdetermined. Consider the following case:

> A tribe has two concepts, akin to our 'pain'. One is applied where there is visible damage, and is linked with tending, pity etc. The other is used for stomach-ache for example, and is tied up with mockery of anyone who complains. [...] I want to say: an education quite different from ours might also be the foundation for quite different concepts. (Wittgenstein 2004: §§ 380, 387)

This imaginary tribe has the same biological nature as other humans, but it has developed different pain-language games and different pain-concepts compared to ours. This kind of conceptual difference in connection with a common human nature is a possibility—and, anthropologists report, often a reality. All humans eat, but the meanings of and rituals surrounding food intake vary greatly. The majority of humans sees colours, but how colours are grouped is not fully identical across the globe. Most cultures have 'coming of age'-rituals, but the content and age of the child varies. This illustrates that language games or moral values and ideals are not derived from facts of nature, and that facts cannot, in themselves, account for the concepts and practices we have (Kuusela 2008: 186; Williams 2009: 11). If human natured changed, so we lost the ability to feel pain, it would most likely lead to a row of changes in our forms of life, but it is an open question *how* our practices would change in response to that. There is thus no justification and exhaustive explanation running from the natural foundations in the bottom of a culture to the higher levels of this culture.

These considerations explain how a universal, for example, biological human nature can be united with the existence of irreducibly different concepts, language-games and cultures. 'Irreducible' does here not mean 'incommensurable' (that we cannot meaningfully compare them). It means that they have a meaning, which is not reducible to the meaning of each other. For instance, a religious practice is different from and cannot be reduced to a scientific one (Wittgenstein 1993a, b). Being human across time and across different cultures does thus not only entail common characteristics, it also always takes on a particular cultural and individual form.

To complicate matters further, even though human nature, like common biological and psychological needs, does not globally cause or explain our moral values, it is often part of what determines what is morally good or bad, and in some situations, we can legitimately refer to, for instance, 'our natural needs', when offering moral justifications. This happens when doctors and psychologists justify recommending breastfeeding or criticise the use of isolation in prisons. What moral values we can honour and create; what cultures we can develop and thrive in depends on nature, both human nature and the nature we are part of. Whatever we succeed with in life, it is always also by 'favour of Nature' (Wittgenstein 2016: § 505). This understanding of the role of nature in morality can be labelled 'non-reductive moral naturalism' or 'normative naturalism' (Crary 2007b: 196–197; Williams 2009).

Yet, what is natural is not necessarily morally good. 'Eye-for-an-eye' seems to express a natural sense of justice among humans. But that is no guarantee that following it will lead to human flourishing. The concept 'natural' is thus not synonym with 'morally good'. If we continue with the example of two tribes with different pain-concepts and -practices, ours and the one Wittgenstein describes earlier, we can ask if the one pain-culture is better than the other is in an ethical sense. Would we be able to give morally convincing arguments to people in this tribe to abandon their practice? Would they be able to present us with ethically compelling reasons for adopting their pain-culture? In order to answer these questions, we would need to know a lot more. But it is not hard to imagine what such reasons could be. Say we found that there was no mental illness in this tribe and say we could establish a reasonable link between this fact and their pain-culture. Would this be considered a good reason to attempt to adopt another pain-culture than our own? It seems so. What if we found that a very high degree of children in the tribe-culture died of diseases, which cause belly pain, but no other visible sign? Then these children would suffer and die while their families were laughing and mocking them. Of course, their parents would do so with the best of intention: They were trying to teach their children not to behave in ridiculous ways as pain behaviour stemming from invisible causes was considered ridiculous. Would this scenario give us reason to evaluate the tribe's practice as morally bad and try to change the tribe's pain culture? I believe that would be an example of what could make us evaluate the practice negatively and where the tribe-members could be said to have good moral reasons to listen to our critique.

In opposition to Posner's earlier claim there are no substantial overlap between different cultures capable of serving as a basis for moral dialogue, evaluation and critique, I have argued that there are common human needs, experiences and vulnerabilities capable to serve as possible sources of trans-historical and trans-cultural moral dialogue, evaluation and critique. We thus have resources for ethical critique both through shared language and shared nature:

> Despite the evident differences in the specific cultural shaping of the grounding experiences, we do recognize the experiences of people in other cultures as similar to our own. We do converse with them about matters of deep

> importance, understand them, allow ourselves to be moved by them [...] there is much family relatedness and much overlap among societies. [...] we do find a family of experiences, clustering around certain focuses, which can provide reasonable starting points for cross-cultural reflection. (Nussbaum 2002: 261, 263, 265)

Posner's claim is that in order for there to be ethically legitimate trans-cultural and trans-historical critique, then there has to be norms and principles for moral judgement universally valid across cultures, according to which we can judge one culture morally better or worse than another. He further claims that no such norms, which are substantial enough, can be found and hence such moral judgements cannot be made. In her work, Nussbaum argues for a critical moral universalism and seeks to balance it with a respect for cultural pluralism (Nussbaum 1998: 1787–1789, 2007: 947). Nussbaum thus seems to accept Posner's premise. She rejects a full-blown ethical contextualism because she deems moral universalism formulated in a moral theory is what can safeguard our ability to morally criticise local moral values, beliefs, traditions and practices (Nussbaum 2001b: 63, 2007: 949–955, 2011: 107, 110–111, 176).

I will not at this point argue for or against the possibility of forms of moral universalism. However, I do want to question that moral universalism formulated in a moral theory is what safeguards a possibility of substantial ethical critique of local traditions and beliefs. It seems to me that the ethical power and legitimacy of a moral critique stems from—for instance—the harm or injustice done, not from it, for example, violating a universal principle. Another way of getting at this is to say that the universal does not automatically have moral priority or takes moral precedence. What is unique to a person or a situation can also raise ethical demands to us. There are strong political, legal and moral reasons to try to figure out what, if anything, is universal for human beings to thrive, and Nussbaum has done important work in this field. But I do believe it is best to reject the assumption that moral universalism and moral theory is necessary in order to safeguard the possibility of trans-historical and -cultural ethical critique.

I argued earlier that the CRC-process illustrates that we can have common moral grounds that allow the giving of moral reasons and justifications across what also are different worldviews, religions and cultures. However, it is relevant to distinguish between degrees of disagreements and conflicts ranging from those were agreement can be reaches, over those were comprises can be made, to irresolvable conflicts. Various cultures and religions have made distinctions in 'the human', distinctions between those worthy of protection and not as worthy of protection, those fully and those not fully human (slaves, embryos, mentally handicapped, people of colour, etc.). The ethical legitimacy of such divisions is an example of what has been and still is hotly disputed.

A trait of morality is thus that disagreement is intelligible and that debates do arise on moral issues to a greater and more violent degree than, for instance, in our practice of mathematics, where it is rare that a physical fight breaks out (Wittgenstein 2009: § 240, II: 237, 2016 § 655). When it comes to moral issues, like also in political, economic and religious matters, we allow debate and conflict to arise more often, and in more ways, than we allow it to arise in basic mathematics and in the following of traffic rules (Christensen 2011: 808–809). It also seems to be a fact about human existence that sometimes conflicts are not resolved. Again, the CRC process is illustrative:

> It was unavoidable that in such a setting some issues could not be settled. These were issues on the 'minimum age' of the child, in other words permitting the outlawing of abortion; the freedom to choose (another) religion, which is prohibited under Islamic law; the protection of children in intercountry adoption; and, the age at which children should be permitted to take part in armed conflict. (Koren 1996: 170)

Even after ten years of intensive work, some moral issues remained a topic of disagreement. In conflicts of a moral nature it happens that we run out of reasons and reach bedrock—the place where our 'argumentative spade turns', and we cannot provide more fundamental reasons or arguments (Wittgenstein 2009: § 217). Sometimes, Rorty reminds us,

> we have exhausted our argumentative resources. Talk of the will of God or of the rights of man, like talk of 'the honour of the family' or of 'the fatherland in danger' [...] are all ways of saying, 'Here I stand: I can do no other'. (Rorty 1999: 83–84)

The nature of this 'standing fast' is not that it is empirically impossible for the person to move, like it is impossible for me to flab my arms and fly or thrive on a diet of dirt and pebbles. It is also not logically impossible. We can imagine a person doing something she in the above sense cannot do—like Sophie could not send her child to death in *Sophie's Choice*. The kind of impossibility, Rorty is dealing with here, I believe, is the kind where we would betray what is most dear to us and will 'lose ourselves', if we move. Sofie could not send one of her children into death. She did. And she was never the same after having done so.

When there is moral difference and disagreements between people, and moral bedrock has been reached, several things can happen: we, for instance, can call the others 'Idiots or Heretics', and thus dismiss the possibility of further meaningful dialogue with them (Wittgenstein 2016: §§ 609–612). We sometimes, as Posner suggests, try to persuade and convert the other party by emotional appeals or by threats. We also go to war or in other ways try to defend our way of life or force the other people to adapt our worldview and values. These latter reactions were what the European settlers did to the Native Canadians, by, for example, outlawing their religious and legal practices and taking their children away to boarding schools where they were not allowed to speak their native language. We also, as Rorty points to and as was the case with the CRC process, sometimes choose to make the best possible compromise and 'agree to differ' on the rest (Rorty 1999: 26). What can and ought to be done when bedrock reaches a moral disagreement cannot be settled in the abstract or according to a universal rule. It depends on each concrete case.

There is political and moral wisdom in Moody-Adam's remarks on the importance of patience in ethical matters. Given ten years and the right institutional and political setting, most of the nations of the world were able to work out a legal document dealing with numerous difficult moral issues. As a reaction to Posner's anti-rationalism, Moody-Adams suggests that we reject the thought 'that if we cannot find definitive solutions to serious moral problems then this renders moral inquiry and argument deficient' (Moody-Adams 2017: 162). The CRC process lends support to that view. In moral life there is a wide range of different forms and levels of disagreement and giving up moral reason-giving and debate on all of them in advance, because some of them might turn out to be irresolvable, seems unwarranted and unwise.

CHAPTER 13

# Moral Uncertainty

What if we simply care about the wrong things? (Delacroix forthcoming: 8)

This simple question is haunting in light of the changes to what we earlier have and have not cared about, what we have and have not believed, and what we have and have not done. The neglect of unwanted children, the stigmatisation and criminalisation of homosexuals, the cruel and unjust treatment of indigenous people, the unneeded harm to animals and so forth. Humans have done so much harm, and much of it with the best of intentions. Why should I—should we be any morally better than those who went before us? How can we trust that we know what is right, good and just? And how can we act, if we cannot have this trust?

Cavell offers us one approach to these questions in the following quote:

> In 'learning language' you learn not merely what the names of things are, but what a name is; not merely what the form of expression is for expressing a wish, but what expressing a wish is; not merely what the word for 'father' is, but what a father is; not merely what the word for 'love' is, but what love is. (Cavell 1999: 177)

Cavell here seems to say to those of us, who doubt our moral judgement and sensitivity, that we *do* know what, for example, 'love' is. The ethically good and bad is something we can point to and give ordinary examples of. To transform Wittgenstein's words from another context: *This* is what love


C. Eriksen, *Moral Change*,
https://doi.org/10.1007/978-3-030-61037-1_13

and taking care amounts to. To take care *is this*. For instance, what you learned from a loving parent or good friend. When we use the word 'know', the way we normally use it (and how else should we use it), then you and other people quite often know what to do to take care of someone, when you have done something wrong or how to fight for justice (Wittgenstein 2009: § 246; 2016: § 47; Hanfling 2003: 25–26). The ethically good and the bad is *this*, visiting your dying friend, taking your anger out on the wrong person. It is normally not something beyond our horizon or in any way hidden. In many cases it is open to see, and it is all around us in our everyday lives. To claim that you do not know what 'love' is, is in other words to betray the nourishment given to you as a child that made you survive, the kindness of the stranger bringing back your lost wallet, the pain of the man mourning his lifelong partner's death, and the affection your small children so undeservedly shower you in on a daily basis.

However, these everyday reminders of what our words mean, how we learned them, and how we have used them are exactly what a moral sceptic cannot acknowledge as ethically relevant and legitimate examples—they represent the problem, not the solution (Prichard 2012: 257). There is an almost scandalous self-righteousness to such everyday reminders. The sceptic exclaims: "I know what we *call* 'morally good', 'bad' and 'justified'. But how is *that* ethically justified? How can we be certain this really are examples of the morally good, bad and justified? With what right do we not doubt this?"

When the moral sceptic worries about what she or we consider morally good, might not really be what is morally good, she implicitly presumes there is a permanent gap between what we call 'morally good' and what is morally good. This implicit assumption is, however, problematic, which I will try to spell out in three different ways.

Firstly, when the sceptic is talking about 'the morally good', 'legitimate', 'trustworthy' and so forth, she is using words from her society's common, public language. If what she says is to have any meaning, she is then either introducing a new meaning to these words or she is accountable to the criteria for using the words found in common language (Hanfling 2003: 27). If the sceptic is introducing a new meaning and is using the word 'morally good' in a completely different meaning than the ordinary one, then this cannot challenge or give us any reason to doubt the legitimacy of our ordinary concept of the good either, because in that case she is simply talking about something altogether different

(Wittgenstein 2009: §§ 480–483). If she is not introducing a wholly new meaning, she is thus still accountable to the common criteria for the uses of her words. If a person is to express a moral critique or an ethical worry, certain conditions must be obtained:

> To suggest that people can 'decide' what methods to use in supporting a moral judgement is to suggest that people can decide what a moral judgement is, can decide whether an issue is a moral one. You may of course decide to *make* a moral issue out of a conflict, but you cannot decide what will be making it a moral issue, what kinds of reasons, entered in what way, to what effect, will be moral reasons. You may decide to use propaganda in the service of a cause. But to call that morality only blinds us to a choice for which we are responsible. You may lie, and worse, and be justified; but why call it noble? (Cavell 1999: 289)

We are not the sole masters of our words if our use of them is to be meaningful—we have to answer to the situation we are in, to language, to reality, to life. If someone in honesty agitates for the right of rocks or socks to have religious autonomy, it would be unclear what he meant. If someone agitated for children to have religious autonomy, we might disagree, but the suggestion would make sense—we have an idea of what that could imply. Children are creatures regarding whom a discussion on autonomy and rights do arise, as we saw in the narrative on *CRC*. Does that mean that it was morally justified and the morally right thing to do, when children were given their own convention in international law? These are not questions that can be answered philosophically, as they ask for moral judgements to be made. What can be said from a philosophical perspective is that these are examples of what have been called morally justified and that it made sense to give children rights. Unlike stones and vira, they are able to 'carry them', to live up to what it means to have 'a right to be heard in matters important to their lives'.

A second way of addressing the sceptical worry is to turn the justification question against the moral sceptic. The moral sceptic seems to know what 'moral justification' and 'morally good' is, when posing her questions. But then she is using the very moral and linguistic resources, which she is questioning the ethical validity of, in order to express her doubts. This makes her worry self-refuting, and the worry is hereby exposed as empty. The sceptical doubt is thus not something that has power to challenge a society's moral ideals or uses of words.

The last way to approach the moral sceptical challenge is to attempt to accept it—accept that we need to ethically justify our practices, concepts, moral ideals and values and demonstrate they are morally trustworthy. How can that be done? It seems that we have to develop a meta-language and a meta-morality containing the criteria for establishing the morally trustworthiness of our ordinary values, criteria, ideals and so forth. Yet this opens the question on how the criteria, concepts, ideals and so forth of the meta-language and meta-morality are justified. Are they in accord with true morality? To answer that question a meta-meta-language and meta-meta-morality would have to be established. But how about the moral justification of that? Is the solution a meta-meta-meta-morality? Clearly not. Accepting the moral sceptic's challenge leads to an infinite regress and absurdity, which is another way of showing the challenge to be flawed (see also Hermann 2015: 12–14). One conclusion to these considerations is to reject the assumption that our morality and our life form is in need of the kind of moral justification, the sceptic is asking for, because it is an empty, flawed request, and maintain that being morally justified (or cruel, kind, generous, etc.) is, under normal conditions, to live up to the criteria of being morally justified (or cruel, kind, generous, etc.) in our language and life form. In line with this, Rorty's response to the person worried about how to trust her and her culture's morality is:

> why should the fact that we use the criteria of our time and place to judge [...] cast doubt on that judgement? What other criteria are available? [...] the contingency of our moral outlook, and its dependence on material conditions, no more impugns our moral superiority than Galileo's dependence on expensive new optical technology impugned the Copernican theory of the heavens. (Rorty 2007: 920)

When haunted by sceptical doubt, we can remind ourselves how we learned the words we use to express ethical concern in our lives, and that can hopefully dissolve our doubts and bring us back to a world where we are able to move and act.

A person in the grip of doubt about her society's moral ideals and values might not be calmed by Cavell, Rorty and other 'ordinary ethics' reminders. Because we *do* sometimes in morally meaningful and non-empty ways say things like: 'He isn't really good, although by the ordinary criteria he is good'. We *can* think of cases where there is an ethical need to move beyond our ordinary understanding of good and bad, just and unjust, like there was for the Crow after they moved to the reservations, for the Native Peoples of Canada to gain acceptance of their land rights, for women in order to be treated with respect and as equals in modern work life and for men in order to be the same in modern family life. Moral critics fights their own and their cultures' vocabularies and moral ideals but do not want to give up the idea of the good. They want to challenge and change what we ordinarily say and do.[1]

I believe we here have to distinguish between two forms of doubt—an empty, sceptical doubt and a genuine ethical doubt. And I further believe Lear's concept of an 'ironic disruption' can cast light on the difference between the two (Lear 2011). According to Lear, ironic disruption happens when we are doing what we are supposed to do as engaged, competent, reflective, prudent, critical and self-critical participants in our practices as, for example, teachers, doctors, Christians, parents, friends or citizens. It happens when we are mature masters of practical judgement in our lives. In this situation we can nonetheless be struck by an unsettling disorientation, a feeling that perhaps '*none of this*' is truly being a parent, a teacher, a citizen or a doctor, that perhaps among 'all the teachers, there never was a teacher', or 'among all the Christians, no Christian' (Lear 2011: 4–24). The ironic disruption is the experience that the ideal of our practice, which we as a matter of how we live are deeply committed to, is calling us to transcend what we understand to be incarnating this ideal. As a result:

> one no longer knows one's way about. [...]. my past continues to be intelligible to me. But I now have this question: What does *any of that* have to

[1] Also philosophers have engaged in meaningful critiques of 'the ordinary'. For example, Nietzsche launched a radical ethical critique and struggled to talk about the good and evil beyond the good and evil of his time (Nietzsche 1993a, b, 1997, 1999a, b, c; Lear 1984: 163; Nehamas 1994; Blok 2010). Kierkegaard can be said to have done the same when it came to Christianity (Kierkegaard 1990, 1994a, b, 1996a, b; Creegan 1989; Phillips 1993; Weston 1999; Lear 2011). For other examples of such creative and critical struggles with ideas and concepts, see Bohr (1985), Baier (1987), Butler (1990), Held (1990), Haslanger (2008), Zigon (2019) and Lear (2008). Moody-Adams also points to one situation where conceptual innovation was called for, namely to describe the evils of the Nazi regime during World War II. About the Nazi's invasion of the Soviet Union in 1941, "Churchill insisted that 'We are in the presence of a crime without a name'. Three years later, with a deeper understanding of the scope of Nazi atrocities, a scholar named Raphael Lemkin coined the word 'genocide' to describe any deliberate and systematic effort to destroy entire groups of people solely because of their racial, national or religious affiliation" (Moody-Adams 2017: 160).

> do with *teaching*? [...] I have lost a sense of how my understanding of my past gives me any basis for what to do next. [...] my experience is not that my act falls miserably short of my principle; rather, my experience is of my principle falling weirdly short of itself. (Lear 2011: 15, 18, 101)

In order to make best sense of the idea of ironic disruption I believe that when it occurs, there is something in one's practice or life, which gives rise to it. The teacher who experiences the disruption might not consciously know what it was that triggered the ironic experience. Was it the brief expression of joy on the face of a child being replaced with disappointment, like a light going out? Was it a vague registering of something not really working socially despite being called 'a solution' by the politicians? Was it a slight unease by teaching certain topics and not others to the children? Was it the dream she had last night, what was it now? The person experiencing an ironic disruption is deeply engaged in her practice, not disengaged, and her doubt is not empty. She is on to something *worth* being attentive to, even though she might lack the words for expressing it clearly. Furthermore, she does not doubt everything, but doubts her practice of teaching. Her disorientation further "manifests passion for a *certain* direction. It is because I care about *teaching* that I have come to a halt as a teacher" (Lear 2011: 19, my italics). This sets ironic disruption apart from sceptical doubts. If the disruption keeps haunting her, she might start a creative struggle with her language, practice and perhaps even culture to try to find a better way of teaching. What this will entail is an open question; it is part of what has to be worked out.

As I see it there is a crucial difference between the moral sceptic and the moral critic, namely that the latter—like Nietzsche, Lear's teacher and the people who developed the idea of paid damages and the concept of sexual harassment (Moody-Adams 2017: 157–158)—is addressing something concrete. Their worry arises out of a specific context and form of life, for specific reasons, and if they peruse their disorientations instead of ignoring it, they will often be able to elaborate their worries in a way we can recognise as ethical worries. This is what the abstract and global worry of the moral sceptic fails in doing, and this is why it poses no real ethical challenge to us, but only the illusion of one. And potentially a harmful one if it develops into an excuse for turning the blind eye to suffering in plain view, and thus into an excuse not to accept responsibility and act.

Yet, Cavell nonetheless writes: "that the skeptic's denial of our criteria is a denial to which criteria must be open" (Cavell 1999: 47). A way of unfolding this remark is to note that the possibility of ironic disruption is something inherent in our practices and in human life. It is part of "the insecurity about being human that is constitutive of being human" (Diamond 2011: 144). The 'must' displayed in the Cavell quote is not a logical or an instrumental must, but an ethical must. It entails an ethical demand and obligation to be attentive to 'the other', to what is alien and unknown to us because at the blurred edges of or even outside the horizon of our worldview, but which nonetheless can have an ethical claim on us. Ethically, we must leave room for uncertainty being able to arise, without it undermining our ability to judge, decide and act.

CHAPTER 14

# Moral Certainty

> It is very difficult to think of traditional values as having any normative authority at all: tradition gives us only a conversation, a debate, and we have no choice but to evaluate the different positions within it. (Nussbaum 2011: 107)

In one caste in India "women are traditionally prohibited from working outside the home—even when, as here, survival itself is at issue. If she [Metha Bai, a young widow with two young children] stays at home, she and her children may die shortly. If she attempts to go out, her in-laws will beat her and abuse her children" (Nussbaum 2001a: 1). Being certain that we are right and thus doing 'what we simply do' has so often turned out to be doing harm and injustice, as it also turned out for Metha Bai and her two children. Nussbaum, therefore, insists on evaluation, debate and active, enlightened choices of traditions as a way of avoiding human harm stemming from too blind a trust in our ordinary ways of doing things.

Yet think of the following case: A small child trips, falls from the sidewalk and is hit by a car. His father runs to him, attends to his wounds, calms him and calls an ambulance. In this situation there is certainty and blind, instinctive reaction. Certainty that there is pain. Certainty that the right thing to do is to tend to the person in pain. "Just try—in a real case—to doubt someone else's fear or pain!" Wittgenstein suggests to his reader (Wittgenstein 2009: § 303). Even just imagining what it would be like to enter such doubt makes it clear that for a bystander to doubt the


C. Eriksen, *Moral Change*,
https://doi.org/10.1007/978-3-030-61037-1_14

boy's pain and ask for a justification of the father's actions would be not only misplaced, but deeply inappropriate. We would most likely call it insane (Pleasants 2008: 163). In this case, there is no room for doubt about the child's pain, and no room for requiring a justification of the father's action—the context for it is wrong.

In this situation, and in countless other situations, doubts do not arise and a 'language game of justification' is not played. "I know that a sick man is lying here? Nonsense! I am sitting at his bedside, I am looking attentively into his face.—So I don't know, then, that there is a sick man lying here? *Neither* the question *nor* the assertion makes sense" (Wittgenstein 2016: § 10, my italics). The kind of certainty, Wittgenstein is drawing our attention to here, is one which characterises the human form of life (Wittgenstein 2016: §§ 204, 358, 359, 475; Moyal-Sharrock 2015: 38; Pleasants 2008: 251). Some of this certainty relates to moral matters, like in the aforementioned case, and Pleasants terms this 'basic moral certainty' (Pleasants 2008: 241).[1]

Moral certainties are part of the earlier mentioned bedrock we reach in moral and moral philosophical debates (Hermann 2015: 3). We reach bedrock, when we cannot give more fundamental or weighty reasons than those we have already given: 'Why do you call torture of children morally bad?' 'Why? What an odd question to ask. Because it is obviously very pain- and harmful to them!' 'But with what right do you consider doing harmful things to children bad?' 'I do. And it does not lend itself to justification'. It does not lend itself to justification, as it is not an open question. "Why do I not satisfy myself that I have two feet when I want to get up from a chair? There is no why. I simply don't. This is how I act." (Wittgenstein 2016 § 148, see also 2001: Part 7 § 40). That harming children is bad is something that 'stand fast' for us and that we use for justifying other things.[2] Nothing is more certain or fundamental than this.[3] Basic moral certainties are part of the framework that allows practices of moral justification to exist and unfold and is itself neither justified nor unjustified (Wittgenstein 2016: §§ 559, 358–359; Christensen 2003:

[1] Pleasants (2008), Prichard (2012), Brice (2013), Brandhorst (2015), De Mesel (2015), Hermann (2015) and O'Hara (2018) are examples of philosophers who use Wittgenstein's work to develop and discuss conceptions of 'moral certainty'.

[2] 'Stand fast' is a translation of Wittgenstein's expression 'fest stehen', which denotes our relation to, for example, basic certainties.

[3] See Pleasant's discussion of what he sees as moral philosophers' misguided attempts at explaining why 'killing is wrong' (Pleasants 2008: 257–265), and De Mesel's discussion of Singer's suggestion that infanticide can be morally warranted for analogous argumentations (De Mesel 2015).

139–140). Basic certainty is not something intellectual or scientific. It is more akin to instinctive behaviour and living. "The danger here, I believe, is one of giving a justification of our procedure where there is no such thing as a justification and we ought simply to have said: *that's how we do it*" (Wittgenstein 2001: Part 3 § 74). Basic certainties are "part of the background against which we engage in more sophisticated language-games" (Williams 2009: 16)— for example, discussing how animals are to be treated in the production of food, how prisons ought to be run, what a just tax-system looks like in world with globally distributed firms and what good parenting consists in.

If we once again look at the birth of the *Convention of the Rights of the Child*, it was created because there were weighty moral reasons for criticising and changing the international legal system as it was, like children being used as soldiers and in prostitution, suffering from malnutrition and separation anxiety during wars and losing their legal rights when fleeing without their parents. For a period of ten years, it was discussed and debated how these problems in the international legal system could be mended. The CRC was the solution given to the problems. Today there is far less discussion of the CRC. From being part of what is up for discussion in the international and national legal systems—from being a fluid part of the legal practice to borrow Wittgenstein's river picture (Wittgenstein 2016: §§ 96–99)—it is now part of the more stable parts of the international legal system and many national legal practices. The CRC today plays the role of a measuring rod, which entails it is used to asses, judge and discuss whether this or that national state treats its children in a legally and morally acceptable way: "The CRC is the benchmark against which governments and their critics judge progress in the field of children's rights" (Archard 2015: 107).

Pleasants argues, and I agree, that we should operate with *degrees* of moral certainty (Pleasants 2008: 255). What is certain for us and has the role as fundamental in our lives sometimes change. It, for instance, is immensely more certain for more people that harming children is bad than it is that the CRC is the best way of protecting children from harm—the latter is still debatable, and might function as a measuring rod in some legal practices, but it is easy to imagine how it could come about that it would cease to have that role, and it does not have that role for all humans.

When Nussbaum writes, "it is very difficult to think of traditional values as having *any* normative authority at all: tradition gives us *only* a conversation, a debate, and we have *no choice* but to evaluate the different positions within it", I believe the image of ethical normativity and of human life this could suggest is too rationalistic and intellectualistic.[4] What is spontaneous in human life is not all bad. And so is also not all that is instinctive, or habitual or traditional. Further, human life not only is not, but also cannot, and from a moral point of view ought not to be characterised by debate, evaluation and informed choice of every value, tradition and practice in one's society. In the vast majority of cases it would not make sense to raise such a debate—as in the case with our instinct of running to and tending to our harmed children. Also doing so (debating, evaluating and choosing) would stunt our inability to act. It would replace life with reflection over life. The ordinary way of acting is to run and tend to our child. This is simply what we do in the overwhelming majority of cases. If we stop and evaluate this way of acting, before proceeding as usual, the child would bleed to death. This is not why we do it (these is no why). But it is how we can see it would be morally disturbed to ask the father to halt and evaluate his proceeding as usual. We evaluate and should evaluate values, traditions and practices, *when there is a reason for it.* It makes no sense to do so in case of the father tending to his son, but all the sense in the world to do so in the case of Metha Bai and her children.

A rejection of the very meaningfulness of entering a debate on a way of doing or understand things with a phrase like 'this is simply what we do' likely has a deeply alarming ring to it for all moral critics. It is the sound of manipulative silencing of opposition, of blind dogmatism, of harmful conservatism, of the wish to continue years and years of power, privilege and oppression. Moral critique has indeed been pushed aside repeatedly this way, and a novel ethical critique rarely seems meaningful, not to ourselves and not to others, when we first try to formulate it. Lack of sense is thus not always a sign of something we should reject and park in the nonsense department.

[4] I write that this is an image this quote *could* suggest, as I doubt Nussbaum, if asked, holds this view of human life, as her early writings suggest otherwise. But modern humans do occasionally get caught up in a rationalistic image of human life, where instincts, habits and traditions are considered suspect if not based on enlightened debate and rational choice or on scientific knowledge and proofs. Being captivated by this image can be problematic because it can have us ask for 'more information' and 'proofs' before being willing to act in cases where we ought to have acted (the opposite default position, captured in the phrase 'shoot first and ask afterward', is from a moral point of view of course equally problematic).

CHAPTER 15

# Moral Distortion

> The second theme that interest us [...] is the thoroughness with which the Nazi regime transformed the conventional moral order, causing its citizens to lose their moral bearings. The Nazis worked with a highly moralized conception of society, based on perverted notions of duty, honor, loyalty, fidelity, and the like. Their behaviour wasn't a matter of amoralism or sheer criminality. (Pauer-Studer and Velleman 2011: 333)

History gives us plenty reason to be worried about how to distinguish between being blind and seeing clearly, between false consciousness and being in contact with reality of things, and so forth. Because of the horrors and apparent 'loos of moral bearings' involved in World War II, in many of the communist regimes and in events like the mass suicide in Johnstown, these worries have surfaced for philosophers, psychologists, anthropologists and social scientists as a preoccupation with figuring out how to prevent people from having too blind an obedience to the dominant norms, traditions, beliefs and laws of their society (Jaeggi 2018: 173–320; Delacroix 2017; Nussbaum 2002: 261, 263, 265; Fuller 1969; Radbruch 1961a, b).[1] As part of this worry thinkers have sought to understand the sources of moral and social criticism: "If principles cannot claim to be

[1] The problem of moral blindness or bias and the conditions and possibilities for critique is also discussed, for example, in Marxist-traditions and in the Frankfurt school, as well as in the many variations of critical legal studies, poststructual, deconstructivist and feminist theory (see, e.g. Hoy 2005; Butler 2002).



C. Eriksen, *Moral Change*,
https://doi.org/10.1007/978-3-030-61037-1_15

constitutively independent from the contingent morass that feeds our ethical sensitivity, where can resistance to our acting as usual spring from?" (Delacroix forthcoming: 2).

But also outside totalitarian regimes and religious sects, humans have trouble figuring out what is good, right and just or only the illusion of the good, right and just. The 'colonial illusions and ghosts' that haunt the Canadian legal officials, laws, courts, parliaments and legislation procedures to some extent blind the people involved. The judge in *Delgamuukw v. The Queen and Registrar*, Judge McEachern, 'had a thin ear' and could not hear Mary Johnson's dirge song and how it proved historical use and stewardship of land (Mandell and Pinder 2012). Such blindness and deafness have made it difficult for the native people to obtain justice. It has even made it difficult to hold on to a language capable of formulating the injustice they suffered. The official story in the legal system and in the broader society for many years was: 'The natives had no *real* law, no *real* political power, no *real* use of the lands, no *real* occupation of the territories, no *real* farming, no *real* ownership'—so, what is even the ethical problem here? If the colonial language is accepted, there is no ethical issue. The stories of children working during the industrialisation also display forms of moral blindness and ethically distorting uses of language. This can be seen in the death of the chimney boy. It was categorised by the authorities as an 'accidental death'. However, given the conditions these children had to work under, it seems more accidental when they did *not* get stuck. The authorities' use of the term 'accidental death' covers this up and thus distorts what was ethically important to see—that these working conditions could and ought to be changed.[2] One of the things that can make it difficult to spot an ethical distortion in a situation is if there is an element of truth in the distorting language use. That was the case with the chimney-boy: Nobody intentionally killed him, not his boss, and no other person in his society. Nobody wanted him dead. In that sense, his death was indeed accidental.

[2] Moody-Adams mentions another case of ethically distorted language use, namely "the 1896 case of *Plessy v. Ferguson*, when the U.S. Supreme Court made two problematic declarations: first, that racial segregation would not violate the constitutional guarantee of equal protection of the law so long as facilities and accommodations were equal, and second that racial segregation was *in no way* a barrier to making accommodations equal. As a result of this decision, the phrase 'separate but equal' became an officially sanctioned tool for legitimizing racial oppression and perpetuating the fiction that racial segregation is a way of realizing genuine equality" (Moody-Adams 2017: 160).

Furthermore, language changes. It changes, so a currently morally neutral word can get an ethical value as part of its meaning (and vice versa). This happened for the words 'smoker' and 'smoking' in Denmark after the 'Smoking Law' was passed in 2007. From having a neutral meaning, it now designates something slightly morally bad. The institution and word 'slavery' also went from having a neutral use to designating something paradigmatically bad (Pleasants 2010: 159; Green 2013a: 480). Today, in history books, in discussions of international law and in articles on moral philosophy, slavery is often mentioned as a practice, which is morally bad, harmful and unjust beyond any meaningful debate (see, e.g. Moody-Adams 2017; Pleasants 2018; Diamond 2019; Archard 2015: 58; Ishay 2008: 12; Bates 2014: 22–25; Appiah 2010). But until not too long ago, and for thousands of years, slavery was a practice considered natural and indispensable by the vast majority of people in many societies (Diamond 2019; Oshatz 2008).

Nussbaum has further drawn attention to the phenomenon that an ethical distortion can affect not only a society's language-use, laws, ideals and institutions, but that also people's emotions and bodily experiences can be ethically distorted. When investigating the life conditions of women in India, Nussbaum found that on many parameters, these women objectively fared worse than their husbands in relation to health, hunger, education, income, physical abuse, status in society, freedom, life lengths expectancies and political influence (Nussbaum 2001a). Yet, in interviews the women did not rate themselves as faring worse than the men. The reasons for this was, Nussbaum found, that they did not fare bad according to the living standards for how women in their culture were supposed to fare. The practical judgement of these women can thus be argued to be severely impaired as a result of their enculturation and worldview, because not even things such as physical pain and suffering from diseases, physical abuse and starvation worked as an important ethical feedback for them, telling them they deserved to fare better and that their society ought to be improved on many parameters (Nussbaum 2001a, b, 2011: 1–16). If not even the pain and humiliation from abuse serves as reliable ethical feedback mechanism, then 'human nature' also seems unfit as a reliable source of ethical critique.

In earlier sections both 'language' and 'nature' were highlighted as possible sources of ethical critique and resistance. Now we are reminded that they can be ethically distorted. How, on this background, can reminders of language use be of any ethical help to us? "How can a form of life be analyzed and criticized as unsuccessful or 'damaged'?" (Jaeggi 2005: 68) in the cases where our feelings, intuitions and bodily reactions as well as our moral concepts and thus a crucial part of the ethical normativity of our society are distorted? History has shown that we as individuals, in our practices and as a society, fail morally. In the past, we have done so not just on a small scale, but in massive ways like having the economy of our societies depend on a practice of slavery for thousands of years. What precludes that our concepts, laws, feelings, institutions, values, intuitions and practical judgement—*all of our ethical normativity*—are morally distorted, as it has been in the past, but we are unable to see it, because our enculturation blinds us? What can yield genuine ethical resistance? Posner's straight answer is that nothing can:

> Moral intuitions don't link up with anything outside of, or common to, all of us. If your intuition about a moral question differs from mine, you cannot tell me to look harder or to look through a microscope or a telescope, or to consult a reputable scientist, or reputable anyone. You cannot show me that my intuition is an illusion, like the apparent movement of the sun or the bent appearance of a stick in the water. There are also no 'crucial experiments', and no statistical regularities, by which to validate a moral argument. And there are no useful 'inventions' embodying moral theory. (Posner 1998a: 1679)

In the following, I will unfold why I believe Posner's views are mistaken and I will do so through a row of reminders in the form of anecdotes, cases from history, everyday life encounters and other philosophers' ponderings on the same issue.

Nussbaum's investigations of Indian women taught us that we cannot always trust that we are able to recognise an ethically relevant feedback from our body in the form of 'bad pain' (unlike good pain, e.g. from growing stronger after a hard workout). However, history also shows us examples of cases where we did recognise a feedback from our biological nature as ethically relevant. This happened with the practice of breastfeeding, which several times around the world has been abandoned for reasons of 'baby health and hygiene', only to be reinstalled years later for the same reasons (see Cunningham 2012: 366–367; Holohan 1987). Today breastfeeding is considered so important that WHO recommends breastfeeding for two years in poor countries, and 'the advantages of breastfeeding' is mentioned in article 24(e) of *the Convention on the Rights of the Child* as something parents and children should be informed about and be supported in. Part of the stress put on breastfeeding is due to fact that babies get significantly sicker and die on other diets, especially among poor people, as they cannot afford the good, expensive baby formulas and lack access to clean water.

Similarly, when women in the 1970s in larger numbers started working outside of the home and on their workplaces experienced what today is termed 'sexually harassed' by some of their male co-workers, they experience discomfort, when it happened (feeling disgust, threatened, anxiety, humiliated, insecurity, disrespect, etc.), even though lacking the right vocabulary for fully elaborating and explaining it (Moody-Adams 2017; Jaeggi 2018: 8). The individual and collective recognition of the legitimacy of reacting to this discomfort was part of the motivational force behind the women's movement. It seems most likely that this complex discomfort has always accompanied unwanted sexual contact from co-workers, even though it was first openly addressed in the legal systems at a certain time and place in history. During history many women have been told and told themselves that this discomfort was not something to fuss about, but an unpleasant part of life to be avoided, if possible, but otherwise ignored and endured like the pain from cold, hunger and childbirth also was. This is another example of getting a bodily feedback—this time of an emotional character—which was ethically alarming and was, in time, able to be recognised as such.

Roth tells an anecdote about how a relation to another person can be part of what lifts a moral blindness and yields a resistance to distorted concepts:

> Consider the story of Tim Zaal as an example of this sort of ethical transition. Zaal is a former racist skinhead who currently works with the Museum of Tolerance in Los Angeles providing educational programs promoting tolerance. Zaal became part of the skinhead movement as a young adult and eventually entered into a relationship with a woman he met through the movement. When the couple became parents, they introduced their son to neo-Nazism early on such that his first words were "nigger" and "kike." Meanwhile, Zaal and his partner were preparing for the Aryan war—hiding thousands of rounds of ammunition under the child's crib, initiating young teens into their Nazi organization, and assaulting gays in the streets. What was the turning point for Zaal? There does not seem to have been any one event that provided the critical moment, but there were a number of interrelated events that led Zaal to begin to see himself and neo-Nazism in a new

> light. One such event occurred when his partner came to suspect that their child might have American Indian ancestry; she insisted that if this were true, she would kill the child herself. This came as a shock to Zaal, as he realized he did not share his partner's willingness to kill the child if he turned out to be of less than "pure" blood. After other incidents involving threats to his son's safety, Zaal began to question his lifestyle. He also came to doubt the justice of the Aryan code, which asked Zaal to take great risks while leaders remained safe from the eye of the law. Within a few years of breaking off the relationship with his partner and leaving the movement, Zaal had begun dating a Jewish woman and volunteering for the Museum of Tolerance. (Roth 2012: 401–402)

Human lives contain not only encounters with other human beings but also with numerous of other living beings. Helen McDonald writes the following about such an encounter in her autobiographical novel *H is for Hawk*:

> Her eyes are narrowed in bird-laughter. I am laughing too. I roll a magazine into a tube and peer at her through it as if it were a telescope. She ducks her head to look at me through the hole. She pushes her beak into it as far as it will go, biting the empty air inside. Putting my mouth to my side of my paper telescope I boom into it: 'Hello, Mabel.' She pulls her beak free. All the feathers on her forehead are raised. She shakes her tail rapidly from side to side and shivers with happiness. An obscure shame grips me. I had a fixed idea of what a goshawk was, just as those Victorian falconers had, and it was not big enough to hold what goshawks are. No one had ever told me goshawks played. It was not in the books. I had not imagined it was possible. I wondered if it was because no one had ever played with them. The thought made me terribly sad. (Macdonald 2014: 113–114)

Lastly, in Denmark, after homosexuality was de-criminalised more and more homosexuals openly showed their sexual orientation by, for example, living together with their partners, walking hand in hand in public and telling co-workers they were gay. Through this and countless other everyday meetings and interactions between homosexuals and the rest of the population, it became apparent that the earlier conceptions of homosexuals as odd, contagious, mentally ill and homosexuality as something 'damaging' in need of criminalisation were wrong and unjust. In the general public's eye, homosexuals turned out to be utterly normal people. They were the patient teacher in primary school, the cranky bus driver, the

American ambassador, and your own dear little sister. The only thing that set homosexuals apart from the majority were their sexual orientation, and it became apparent that was not something harming anyone more than a heterosexual orientation was.

What these anecdotes testify to is that meetings and interactions between humans and between humans and other living beings can yield moral resistance and disrupt the concepts and values on both the level of individuals and of whole societies as well as being something motivating the development of new concepts, practices and institutions.

Considered as a race, the human is a social animal—the vast majority of us live in groups—and we even live in groups within groups. Being brought up in communities not only at times supplies us with an ethically distorted way of thinking and living, but it also supplies us with a wealth of sources for ethical critique and disruption. Moody-Adams points to one such source in social hierarchies. In the overwhelming majority of societies, people have different statuses and occupy different roles. These differences in status and roles create experiences and insights, which can be a source of and give rise to ethical critiques of society (Moody-Adams 2002: 68–69). This may be as 'voices from the margin', as was the case with the Native Canadians. When parts of the Canadian legal and political system were and are influenced by harmful illusions, the people suffering the most under these illusions—and in this case with a historical experience and knowledge of it *being* illusions—fight back (see also Zigon 2019 for an example of this). But ethical critique arises not only from the margins of society. It can also arise from good and bad experiences with living in the midst or the top of the hierarchy. The Russian author Tolstoy was not overly impressed with what he considered the inauthentic and shallow form of life of the upper class in his society, to which he himself belonged, and he created ethically rich, world literature based on these experiences and insights—like the novella *The Death of Ivan Ilyich* about a man who in his obsession with the perfect décor of his home happens to fall from a chair and sustains an injure, slowly killing him and leaving him lonely, as all his social peers cannot handle the unpleasant reality of death.

Besides hierarchies, there is also the phenomenon of 'sub-cultures' within a society (Sen 2007; Nussbaum 2011). Many human beings are members of several social groups within their society, each with their own social hierarchy, beliefs and values. Besides being a member of her society, a child in a typical western society, can thus also be a member of a 'core-family', an extended family with grandparents, aunts and uncles, a school-class, a school, a group of friends in the neighbourhood, a sports-team, a church, a village and political youth organisation. Her social position and her experiences will most likely vary across these memberships, so she can be 'low caste' in her national-society, but the leader of her soccer team, the best of her school-class, and an 'average-Jane' in the youth-organisation. These varied memberships of different groups and practices can provide an individual with experiences and different concepts, ideals and worldviews that can help lift moral blindness and fuel a critique of other parts of her society. Subcultures, social groups, practices and so forth "are not singular units, closed off from one another. They overlap in ways that make it possible to use the resources from one practice to scrutinize another" (Christensen 2015: 44).

Furthermore, only very rarely a society is sealed off from contact with other societies and cultures (Nussbaum 2011; Sen 2007: xii, 19; Moody-Adams 2002; Diamond 2012, 2013). Trade, travel, missioning, war, politics and migration have, as far back as we have historical evidence, lead to trans-cultural exchanges. These encounters and exchanges can also supply us with rich resources for ethical critique and development of our own society. The Native Canadians furthered their cause by making other nations and the UN aware of their struggle through the media. They were helped by the international society criticising Canada's government, and they were further helped through international law-making protecting their rights. International law offered another language than the national 'colonial language', which supported the Native Canadians in the formulation of, as well as the legal and ethical legitimacy of, their legal claims. The worry about our cultures, languages and conceptual worlds being sealed spheres, which could be ethically distorted, so we were doing evil without having any chance of recognising it, is misguided and also rests on an over-simplified picture of the character of a culture. 'Societies', 'cultures', 'lifeforms' and so forth are not something we in any way should understand in analogy to either homogeneous or sealed spheres. They are often not even to be understood as something having a boundary, not even a porous one, setting an inside and outside to the culture (Diamond 2013). Nussbaum summarises the nature of cultural complexity through the metaphor of voice: "we should bear in mind that no culture is a monolith. All cultures contain a variety of voices" (Nussbaum 2011: 106).

The last trait of living in a community and being enculturated, I want to draw attention to here, which can serve as a source of ethical critique and creativity, is that to be raised as a human entails the learning of the a language, the moral and social rules, taboos, laws, obligations, ideals, values, and so forth of one's society. All of this involves learning to be reflective and evaluative in the use of them. This is so because laws, words, norms, rules and so forth cannot apply themselves, only we can. Clearly, the amount of effort involved in this application differs. Some rules we generally follow blindly, after having first learned them, like when adding 2 to any number, when stopping at a red light, and when answering what colour the light we stop at is. But if a toddler just ran out in front of my car, this (hopefully) would stop my automatic 'drive' response, when the light turns green. In other cases, reflection and the use of practical judgement is regularly involved, like when figuring out how to react 'dignified' when treated unjustly ('when they go low, we go high', Michelle Obama advices us). To learn how to use a word or follow a law is, at the same time, learning to judge how, when and if it is, for example, meaningful or justified to apply or follow it. This in itself creates a critical potential towards the concepts, laws, values and ideals of one's society, and an ability to spot when the world has changed, so our laws, norms or ideals no longer apply or are apt to navigate in it (Morawetz 2000a: 20; Christensen 2011: 808–809; Delacroix 2017). To be enculturated is thus always also to develop an ability for critical reflection, which can also serve as a tool for detecting moral distortion.

In this section we have looked into examples of how moral blindness has been lifted and ethical distortions have been spotted. However, moral blindness is still a puzzling phenomenon. When reading about the life of children in, for instance, Europe, it seems that for thousands of years, an often extreme physical, social and psychological abuse and suffering of some groups of children existed in plain sight. But it was not until the mid-nineteenth century that the sufferings of these children were seen as something presenting an ethical demand for not just charity workers, but for effective political action and the public at large. *Was* the suffering really there to be seen all along? Or did it only come into existence *as* suffering, when conceptions of childhood changed? Or was it there all along, but it was *impossible* for people to see it? Philosophers disagree over these matters.

On the moral revolutions, Appiah investigates, he notes: "Duelling was always murderous and irrational; footbinding was always painfully crippling, slavery was always an assault on the humanity of the slave" (Appiah 2010: xii). The moral change that happened, when we abandoned these practices, was thus not a change in what is good or bad for humans. What changed was our understanding of this moral reality. The evil of slavery was there all along to be seen and recognised. A similar view and understanding of moral change can be found in Moody-Adams: "the ancient Greeks didn't need any new moral ideas—certainly not the Enlightenment ideal of equality, for instance—to be able to recognize and condemn the moral wrong of ancient slavery" (Moody-Adams 1999: 182). According to Moody-Adams, moral changes are not changes of moral reality or of our moral values, ideas or concepts, but only changes of our understanding of them (Moody-Adams 1999: 168, 169, 2017: 2–3, 9). When she explains why we earlier failed to see moral reality clearly, she points out that "moral failures of past societies cannot be explained by appeal to ignorance of new moral ideas, but must be understood as resulting from refusals to subject social practices to critical scrutiny" (Moody-Adams 1999: 168). The latter unwillingness has often to do with selfish economic interests (Pleasants 2010: 162, 163).

Another explanation is that people are not unwilling, but not *able* to discover their own ideology, false consciousness and moral blindness. It was impossible, for example, for the stoics to think and discover that slavery is wrong (Annas 2011: 60), and for Danes, in the 1920s, to think that consuming meat and dairy products was in any way morally problematic, because they lived in societies that was heavily dependent on respectively slavery and animal food production and had been so for hundreds of years (Christensen 2015: 46).

If taken as general explanations for all cases of moral blindness, both views seem untenable, though I believe they each can explain some cases of moral blindness: that either people could not have been unable to form critical views or that people were unable to form a critical judgement because of their enculturation (Pleasants 2010: 165). Pleasants offers us a third explanation. He agrees with Appiah and Moody-Adams that ignorance of slavery as harmful for the slave was not the explanation of former time's moral blindness and inability to imagine slavery abolished. But it also cannot be generally explained by unwillingness based on people's selfish greed or by a complete inability to be critical towards their own culture. He finds it more likely that many people:

> looked upon the plight of slaves rather as most of us now look upon the world's starving: registering the badness of their situation while regretting that there is nothing that *we* can do about it. [….] [Today we accept] animal exploitation, consisting mainly in the institutionalized practices of breeding,

> killing, and vivisecting animals for food production and knowledge accumulation. [...] [Nowadays mostly passive] sympathy for the suffering of animals sits alongside an unshakeable belief in the naturalness, necessity, and justness of the practices themselves. (Pleasants 2010: 165, 166)

According to Pleasants, a better explanation for the "profound transformation in moral perception" when it comes to slaves can be found in the removal of practical, social and economic barriers, that hereto had made slavery seem indispensable for societies (Pleasants 2010: 160). In order for people to change their view of harmful practices, which they have been brought up to consider indispensable for their own security, wellbeing or utility, a realistic alternative in the form of a different practice had to be developed (Pleasants 2010: 169).

I find Pleasants' explanation convincing for many cases of moral blindness and moral change on a societal level. One of its strengths is that it does not turn the majority of people in the past into 'morally witless' persons (as in the 'ignorance of the suffering in slavery'-explanation), or into 'selfish assholes' (as in the 'will not see because of greed'-explanation), and lastly, it also does not make all moral change wholly coincidental (as the 'critique was completely impossible'-explanation seems to do). Before the mid-nineteenth century, it was thus not impossible to compare a rich and a poor child. Rather the claim is that they *were* not generally compared in this way, *and* it would not have made much sense to people if it was done, among other things because it was conceived to be 'the natural order of things' that some kids were poor and others not (see Christensen 2015 for a similar argument about slaves). If we look back at the report by the work-colleague of the chimney-boy, who suffocated during their work shift, then his account strikes me as displaying both a quiet sorrow, a discomfort with his and others inability to help the boy when he was stuck, and a deep resignation towards the suffering he is witnessing, which resonates well with Pleasant's explanation of moral blindness. Also, the narrative of how the practice of feuds was replaced by a compensations-system also supports Pleasant's claim that one road to moral change is to develop a realistic alternative in the form of a different practice. This does not preclude that we can also find cases were moral blindness can be explained by lack of knowledge, greed, selfishness, brainwash or something else, and that in these cases other roads to moral change should be found.

To return to general worry touched upon in the introduction to this section, that we might be morally deluded without being able to find out,

I believe this worry rests on a misguided idea of the nature of moral blindness and ethical distortions; something which Lear captures in one sentence: "if we are to give content to the idea of something's being an illusion, we need to give content to the idea of our coming to recognize it as illusion" (Lear 2011: 8). This is a remark on the concept of 'illusion'. It is logically linked to a concept like 'reality'. And that can be extended to the concepts of 'false consciousness', 'morally blindness', 'ethical distortion' and so forth. It is true that we can be morally blind and that our society in major respects can be ethically distorted. But in these cases, we can, necessarily so, also come to realise that this is the case. Otherwise, we are simply not dealing with blindness, illusion or distortion. Reality is what has the ability to kick back and yield resistance to our too narrow conceptions of what reality is—to what being a child, homosexual, woman, slave or goshawk entail. The fear that we could suffer from moral blindness without ever being able to find out is thus an empty worry. The worries that 25 children in kindergarten classes do not thrive with only two adults to take care of them, that animals and the environment might suffer too much from our current food production, that migration threatens the social stability of Europe, that the use of AI threatens the rule of law, or that waging a war on drugs might not solve any drug-related problems are not empty worries.

What I want to conclude is that there are ways we can come to realise something is ethically amiss with us and with our society. We can become morally less blind, discover our moral mistakes and have the grip of a distorted ethical normativity in our society loosened in various ways: through art, experience, language, nature, culture meetings, coming to care about something, meeting another person, through knowledge of history—all of this, and countless other things, can be sources of genuine ethical critique and 'resistance to or acting as usual', as well as reservoirs of ethical creativity. Delacroix's and Jaeggi's questions allow of no final or universal answers. They allow of an incomplete, because incompletable, row of reminders.

Such gestures to history, to anecdotes, to everyday life and to philosophers' ponderings admittedly all seem too small and insignificant in the light of the challenges discussed earlier. I believe that what these gestures testify to, like seeds of dandelions, contain more vitality than their frail appearance reveals at first sight. However, none of the sources of ethical critique can stand morally on their own in the sense that none of them offers us a privileged source of moral truth or an incorruptible moral platform to stand on. All of them can become ethically distorted. Moral laurels offer no rest.

> Human beings have always fallen short of the prevailing conception of love. There have always been rebels. Conflicts have never been lacking. (Løgstrup 2020: 75)

The problem of failing morally is not one that can be solved or removed from human life (Cavell 1989: 54, 57). It is a condition we have to learn how to handle and live with.

CHAPTER 16

# Moral Revolution

> Now can I prophesy that men will never throw over the present arithmetical propositions, never say that now at last they know how the matter stands? (Wittgenstein 2016: § 652)

Today it stands fast for us that 2 + 2 = 4, and we cannot make sense of the thought, that this is not a valid calculation. It also stands fast for us that harming children should be avoided. At least, in normal contexts such things stand fast for us: "It is only in normal cases that the use of a word is clearly laid out in advance for us; we know, are in no doubt, what we have to say in this or that case" (Wittgenstein 2009: § 142). In normal contexts the moral evaluation of an action is often, though not always, transparent (Moody-Adams 1999: 170). It is thus normal to know how to bring joy to one's children, and that doing so is a good thing and normal not to know how best to break up one's marriage and being in doubt if one should do so. However, life can also contain 'abnormal situations and contexts', like when we became able to clone humans, and when brain scanners made it possible for us to distinguish between 'dead' and 'brain dead'. Here novel territories were entered and questions of right and wrong were much less transparent. An extensive example of this we saw in the narrative of the Crow. The traditional moral framework and worldview of the Crows to a large extent crumbled, and they lost most of the tools and criteria they had for ethically understanding and evaluating people and situations. The answer to the aforementioned question in the Wittgenstein



C. Eriksen, *Moral Change*,
https://doi.org/10.1007/978-3-030-61037-1_16

quote must be 'No. Of course not'. It is a possibility and a fact about human life that radical changes and revolutions happen on an individual as well as a cultural level, and in math as well as in morality. Changes of a whole form of life thus in a new way raise questions of trans-historical moral evaluation—if our very criteria and measuring rods for ethical evaluation have changed, how can we compare the old and the new form of life? It seems we cannot. But then we cannot justify calling any moral revolution an example of moral progress, and that does also not seem right.

The topic of this section is on radical changes and not only moral revolutions. A moral revolution is a, or several, radical changes. Not any radical change is a revolution. I could convert to a fundamentalist religion, and this would be a radical change in my life, but we would most likely not refer it as a revolution. I have nonetheless chosen to name the section 'moral revolutions' as this is a popular term often used to discuss the topics of this section. In the following, two intertwined issues will be discussed. The one is whether it makes sense to speak of radical moral changes. The other is whether trans-historical moral evaluation of radical moral changes is possible, or if there is 'moral incommensurability' in these cases.[1]

The discussion of radical moral change and incommensurability has two extremes. At the one end we find proponents—like Posner and Rorty—of the view that history has breaks, and that we cannot morally evaluate or justify across these radical discontinuities between shifting 'final vocabularies' in any morally objective way (Posner 1998a; Rorty 2007: 922). When radical moral change happens, it is the result of, for example, the creative minds of charismatic moral entrepreneurs inventing new social roles and dreaming up new interesting possibilities (Posner 1998a: 1674–1690; Rorty 1999: 34; 2007: 922). At the other end we find thinkers like Moody-Adams, who claim that despite the fact that all cultures change over time, radical moral changes do not occur. There cannot be any major 'moral news' and no 'fresh evidence or discoveries', like the invention of truly new moral ideas. Moral invention and discovery are a myth (Moody-Adams 2002: 49, 102, 109, 142; 1999: 170).

[1] As mentioned earlier, the term 'incommensurable' is often associated with Kuhn's work on scientific revolutions and paradigm shifts (Kuhn 1970). The term means 'to have no common measure'. For a critique of the use of Kuhn to understand moral revolutions, see Palmer and Schagrin (1978). For a positive use, consult, for example, Baker (2019), Pleasants (2018), Kitcher (2011) or Appiah (2010).

> Morally speaking, there is never anything 'new' in a new historical epoch. Rather, new and different ways of articulating and interpreting fundamental moral ideas can illuminate features of the moral world obscured or disguised by old interpretations. [...] Novelty in morality and moral inquiry [...] never occurs in basic concepts but only in the reordering and reinterpretation of significant details. (Moody-Adams 2002: 8, 191)

According to Moody-Adams, moral change in the form of moral progress happens when humans acquire a better understanding of existing moral concepts and of 'the structure of moral experience'—and when they use their deepened understanding to improve their behaviour and social institutions (Moody-Adams 1999: 168–170; 2002: 233). As earlier mentioned, she also refers to this as an expansion of our understanding of conceptual space, as deepening our grasp of already existent, complex moral ideas (Moody-Adams 2017, 1999: 170). Trans-historical reflection, evaluation and justification are always possible as human moral concepts, beliefs and principles have essentially stayed the same—only 'secondary moral details' vary between different times and different cultures (Moody-Adams 2002: 16, 61, 62, 80, 106).[2] "Cultural boundaries are not morally impenetrable walls. Neither, however, are the boundaries of historical eras" (Moody-Adams 2002: 61). One of Moody-Adams' arguments against the existence of radical moral change is the following: There can be no radical different morality, because we can only recognise a different morality as such because there is a lot in common between the two moralities (Moody-Adams 2002: 55, 57).

> an unfamiliar judgement or belief can be a moral judgement or belief—and can be recognized as such—only if it fits into a complex set of beliefs and judgements that strongly resembles one's own 'familiar' set. (Moody-Adams 2002: 7)

> New moral insights can be 'assimilated' only if they can somehow be expressed in terms of familiar moral concepts. (Moody-Adams 1999: 170)

Both monogamy and polygamy share a fundamental moral concern for the caretaking of children, and are thus not radically different,

[2] This position sounds like a version of strong moral realism in the tradition from Plato, but Moody-Adams criticises moral realism. She labels herself an 'anti-relativist' and advocates for 'a limited critical pluralism' (see, e.g. Moody-Adams 2002: 8, 203).

incomparable forms of life. The radically alien human form of life does not exist, and revolutionary changes does not occur (Moody-Adams 2002: 59, 109).

I believe both extremes—the view that there are historical breaks, which render before and after in every aspect incommensurable, as well as the view that there are no radical moral changes—are untenable. Once again, a far more complicated picture needs to be drawn in order to gain an understanding of the normativity of radical moral changes. An example of such a complex picture can be found in Lear's narrative of the destruction and rebirth of the Crow form of life.

Moody-Adams' arguments against the possibility of her definition of radical moral change come across as convincing. If the concept of a 'moral revolution', 'moral paradigm shift' or 'radical moral change' has a sense, it cannot be the one Moody-Adams is criticising. Nothing can be a radical change in *that* sense, as that is an empty idea. If we call something a moral change, then we have to be able to recognise what is on both sides of the change as something in some way related to what we call 'morality'.[3] If there is no resemblance at all, then why call it a moral change, and not a soft ice or covfefe? Wittgenstein at one point considers how we would understand the change, if we changed our measuring practice so that instead of measuring rods of wood and metal we started using ones of very soft rubber (Wittgenstein 2001: Part 1 § 5). An interlocutor in his text annoyed responds: "But that would not be measuring at all!" Wittgenstein's answer is that such a practice has enough likeness with our practice for it to make sense to call it 'measuring'. I believe something similar can be the case with ideals and concepts that have a moral use. We can imagine gradual changes from our current concepts up to a point, were there we could no longer say that "there is enough likeness to call it 'caring', 'love', 'justice', etc.", but were would say 'this is something altogether different'. I will argue we can talk meaningfully about radical moral change and incommensurability in a non-empty, yet less extensive sense than the one Rorty and Posner seems to embrace.

Should the changes which the Crow's form of life underwent be described as 'a complete break in history'? What happened was certainly a change; or far better, many changes of various degrees and kinds unfolded, some of them of a moral nature: The telos of their form of life and many

[3] Lear (1984: 165) makes a similar argument for the concept of 'human flourishing' in different societies.

fundamental moral beliefs, ideals, practices and concepts were emptied of value and meaning and disappeared, like 'the meaning of life is hunting and warfare', 'counting coups', 'intertribal war' and 'conquering horses from other tribes'. Some beliefs, concepts, practices, values and ideals stayed or reappeared, but in very changed forms like 'the Chickadee', 'courage', 'dignity', 'strength' and 'the sun dance'. With others, we can say they in some ways stayed the same, like 'raising children', 'the importance of leadership', 'cooking' and 'taking care of the sick'. And we find ethical issues at stake before, during and after the change—young people continued to do stupid things, and the old people still had to figure out how to best deal with this. Therefore, it is not justified to see the change their form of life underwent as 'a complete break in history'. If the changes which the Crow's form of life underwent was not a complete break in history, should we then rather describe them as 'a reordering and reinterpretation of significant moral details'? I believe that would be an odd, and perhaps even disrespectful, description. I will try to argue that the Crow did develop what can be called 'new moral values' and further, that some of the changes, which the Crow form of life underwent, fleshes out what a non-empty concept of 'radical moral change' can amount to.

If we first turn to some of the values and aspects of life, which to the highest degree stayed the same, like 'birth', 'care for children and the sick', 'the importance of cooking' and 'dealing with death', then although they stayed the same in one sense, they did not in another sense. Nothing was the same. The confusion the women felt surrounding these everyday tasks bear witness to this (Lear 2008: 60, 57). It is not the same to raise children, when you no longer know why you do so, what the meaning of your and your children's life is, what excellent living in this world amounts to, and what is worth striving for, besides bare survival. To lack concepts for how to understand the world you have become part of, losing the meaning of your, your family's and community's life, losing most of your land, freedom, legal system, societal status, the right to exercise your religion freely and so forth—this is, if anything is, a massive and in some aspects radical moral change.

If we look at the changes of the ideals and concepts of 'dignity' and 'courage', the Crow used known resources when developing them, like the mythical figure of the Chickadee, as a bridge to build other conceptions of courage and dignity. There are enough likenesses between the concepts to call both conceptions 'courage' and 'dignity'. Nonetheless, I think it makes perfect sense to say that the Crow developed new concepts and values. Even though a horse buggy is a form of transportation, and the airplane is so too, the development of the airplane is an example of what we call an invention: it is a new form of transportation. Likewise, the Crow developed new concepts of 'courage' and 'dignity'. If we imagine a Crow living before the nineteenth century had been presented with the developed concepts, then it is far from certain she would have been able to recognise what these ideas had to do with 'courage' and 'dignity'—that not die fighting but instead cooperate with the enemy could be dignified behaviour. This only made sense on the background of the events and the changed reality for the Crow after 1800. She would have to hear about, perhaps even live through, this part of history for it to make sense (and even then, it is still a debatable issue; the Sioux viewed this topic differently, as we will hear further). Yet, if one has experienced the number and military power of the colonisers, if co-operation gave advantages over one's arch enemy the Sioux, if co-operation contained the hope of holding on to one's land instead of losing it all and if one firmly believed the divine powers have send a dream to one's tribe with a "call to tolerate the collapse of ethical life" (Lear 2008: 92), as well as a recommendation to learn a new way of being courageous and strong, then it is possible to begin to make sense of the idea that there is no dishonour in leaving the old ways behind, and 'courage' and 'dignity' could attain new meanings.

The case of the Crow thus exemplifies how a form of life can undergo changes, where also major parts of the moral framework of a people changed and thus the moral measuring-rods, criteria and ideals, which they had normally used. In cases of radical change, it becomes possible to doubt and criticise those moral ideals and beliefs, we under normal circumstances do not and cannot doubt, because doubt in that context lacks sense (Wittgenstein 2016: §§ 96–99, 192; Crary 2007c: 113–116).

If we turn to the change of life-telos that the Crow underwent, then this, I would argue, is a radical and thus incommensurable change. It is a change from 'For all of us all of life is about hunting and war' to a life where the answer to the question of what life is about for the Crow cannot be answered in any simple way. Lear's story does not tell what the Crow answer today is. I assume that the telos of 'Crow life' is now a fairly open question, something not entirely given, but which to a larger degree has to be worked out, like it seems to be for most people living in the West. The narratives in *There There*, if they can be taken as representative, suggests it is:

> An Urban Indian belongs to the city, and cities belong to the earth. Everything here is formed in relation to every other living and nonliving thing from the earth. [...] Being Indian has never been about returning to the land. The land is everywhere or nowhere. (Orange 2018: 11)

If 'being Indian' today has to do with a relation to the land, and the land is something which is 'everywhere or nowhere', then even though this gives a certain orientation and directs your attention to something rather than other things, it is still a fairly open question what being Indian is about.

Despite the changes the Crow form of life underwent are not as radical as Wittgenstein's Bosch-world-change (mentioned in Part I), I nonetheless think it is unclear how we could evaluatively compare the life telos and form of life of the two and decide whether the one, for instance, is better than the other; an unclarity which can be seen as incommensurability. Even if we grant thinkers like Aristotle and Nussbaum that a universal standard for judging forms of life is how well they allow people 'to flourish', then there still seems to be no straightforward general answer to *this* question in *this* case, if the question is something along the lines of 'is it a better life for humans to live a modern life than the traditional life of the Crow before 1800?'. People having lived in both worlds could have an answer for what they found 'the better form of life', but their answers are probably not unison. Counting Coups might have preferred the old world. I, for one, cannot help worrying, how stressful a life focussed on war and conflict with neighbouring tribes would be—and how it was to be a girl, and later an adult woman in a culture where it was mainly up to the young boys to dream and the old men to interpret the visions for the life of the society.

In his narrative of the Crow, Lear is morally evaluating aspects of the change, they went through, with a use of concepts like 'good', 'shameful', 'genuine', 'courage', 'justification' and 'legitimation' in his description of what happened during and after this change (see, e.g. Lear 2008: 51, 65, 98, 107, 115, 135). His focus is not on deciding which form of Crow life is better, before or after. His focus is on how best to handle major and radical changes of life. The book is a philosophical investigation of what a legitimate hope for the good can look like during the destruction of one's form of life: "the book will examine Plenty Coups's hopefulness—what it was and what might justify it" (Lear 2008: 51). Lear therefore, as I read him, represents an alternative to (or synthesis of) Posner's, Rorty's and Moody-Adams' ways of thinking about radical moral change. He can agree with Posner and Rorty that radical changes in some form can occur, and that new moral vocabularies can be developed. Yet he can also agree with Moody-Adams that there are similarities across changes in forms of life and that we in various ethically legitimate ways can evaluate trans-historically and trans-culturally; for instance, that there are ethically better or worse ways of living through a radical change of form of life. The two tribes and their handling of cultural devastation is an example of what Nussbaum calls 'competing responses to common human problems we encounter in our lives with each other, where we can compare them and see what it might be to act well in the face of these problems' (Nussbaum 2002: 248). The story of the Crow shows us an example of what an ethically good way of facing cultural devastation can look like. The story of Sioux shows us what less good ways of doing so can entail.[4]

Wittgenstein claims that when something is fundamental in our lives, then this entails we can and might choose to hold on to it, even when facing a radical challenge to it. Earlier, Wittgenstein asked what would happen to our practices of justifying claims of knowledge if the world suddenly changed into a mad Hieronymus Bosch world.[5] His own surprising answer is: Not necessarily anything. The world can change radically, yet we chose to 'stay in the saddle' of our practices and continue reasoning as before (Wittgenstein 2016: §§ 612, 616, 619). The reason for this is that we are not forced to change our fundamental ways, because this is what it *means* that they are fundamental to us (Wittgenstein 2016: §§ 245, 512). If something happened, which could cast everything we know of the world into doubt, we could also doubt our perception of the world: Wonder if we were dreaming, had been drugged, gone temporarily mad, or if humans were being tested by God and now had to prove their faith by not letting go of their old ways (Wittgenstein 2016: § 71; Wittgenstein 1997: 56–58). When being reminded of the possibility of these latter reactions, it actually

[4] As mentioned, Lear is presenting us with a narrative inspired by historical events and is not claiming to present the historical truth about the matter (Lear 2008: 7–8). Nonetheless it can cast light on what acting well or not so well during radical changes can entail. The moral judgement here is thus on 'possible ways of acting', and not the Crow and the Sioux as such.

[5] "What if something *really unheard-of* happened?—If I, say, saw houses gradually turning into steam without any obvious cause; if the cattle in the fields stood on their heads and laughed and spoke comprehensible words; if trees gradually changed into men and men into trees. Now, was I right when I said before all these things happened "I know that that's a house" etc., or simply "that's a house" etc.?" (Wittgenstein 2016: § 513).

seems more likely and rational that at first we *would* have that reaction (choose to stay in the saddle), rather than cast everything away. This is so because the reasons and evidence we have for doubting everything are more worthy of doubt themselves (Wittgenstein 2016: §§ 125, 516; Wittgenstein 2004: § 393).

I believe the Sioux's reaction to the colonisation is an example of such a 'stay in the saddle-strategy'. For a long time, the Sioux held on to their old way of life, and their traditional understanding of courage, dignity and strength, by continuing war and physical battles with the government. Sitting Bull, the Sioux chief, regarded Plenty Coups as "a gullible sap or, worse, a collaborator with malign forces. Either way he exercised poor judgement" (Lear 2008: 107). For the Sioux there was no dignity to be found in collaboration—it was a faith far worse than what they saw as the courageous death on the battlefield. Here we have a disagreement over the moral evaluation of a course of actions in a certain historical context. Was the Sioux right in holding on to their old ways and the Crow wrong?

I do not think that this is a question that can be answered definitively in the sense that further discussion of it becomes meaningless—like we can open a box and see if there is or is not a beetle in it, and what we find will in most cases end the discussion for good. Part of the explanation for this is that people can live in different ways and we can say, 'there is good and bad in each way', thus not being able to form one unified judgement over the different forms of life. Another part of the explanation for this is "that it is profoundly difficult to construct a reliable description of the moral practices of an entire *culture*—a description of the sort that could license judgements contrasting one culture's basic moral beliefs with those of other cultures" (Moody-Adams 2002: 41). If we further do not only want to take beliefs into account but everything that is involved in a culture and form of life, things would become even more complicated. A form of life can be morally good and bad in so many ways according to so many different important moral parameters that making a moral judgement over an entire form of life in many cases is either impossible or makes no sense. However, Lear does provide us with reasons for regarding the Sioux's way of dealing with their situation as in some ways morally flawed and as the ethically less good road to take (which is not the same as judging the entire Sioux form of life).

Aristotle understands courage as the virtuous way of handling the basic phenomena of fear and trust in human life (Aristotle 1976: Book 3, Part 6). If we follow him in this, then in order for a battle and war to be meaningful and courageous and not an overconfident and reckless response to a situation, it seems to require the possibility of winning. The Sioux overestimated their own 'battle-power', when they believed that they could win a war against the government. This means that the Sioux leaders were out of touch with an important aspect of reality (this is clear to see in hindsight and a difficult task to get right at the time). Sitting Bull could ask: "If Plenty Coups was courageous, why didn't he choose to go down fighting [...]? [Lear's answers is]: Because Plenty Coups *correctly* saw that dying such a way would no longer be a fine death; and thus avoiding such a death should no longer count as shameful" (Lear 2008: 110). A fundamental precondition for acting morally well is to be in touch with and acknowledge reality. In this case, this is a profoundly difficult task: It entails to accept the destruction of one's form of life, to let go of one's understanding of almost everything, to embrace extreme uncertainty and not cling on to vain forms of hope.

The Crow judged that they could not win the battle against the Europeans in the form of war—that in terms of that kind of power they were facing a superior force. They were right about this. The Crow were outnumbered, and the weapons of the enemy were far more destructive. The world had changed in ways, which made battle in the form of physical war a bad answer to their challenges. In the same way, to continue planting coup sticks as a way of marking territory or stealing horses from other tribes as an attempt to demonstrate courage had become ridiculous and embarrassing ways of acting in the new world and demonstrated a lack of understanding of social reality (Lear 2008: 88–89).

Sitting Bull was also out of touch with 'the spiritual reality', as he misinterpreted the dream visions he received. Sitting Bull had a vision he believed told the Sioux that they had to dance a ritualistic dance, 'the Ghost Dance', and that would turn things around for them. In the entire fall of 1890, the Sioux tribe made it the purpose of life to dance the Ghost Dance (Lear 2008: 150). Why is this misinterpretation and misapplication of a vision? What justifies such a claim? Lear's response seems to be that the ethical flaw in Sitting Bull's interpretation was that it relied on magic—that the world would change to their benefit without the Sioux engaging with the actual problems in their life and without taking any realistic and practical steps to bring better times about (Lear 2008: 150–151). 'Just dance and everything will be all right'. That attitude is not a manifestation of hope but of wishful thinking. It is not an engagement with life, but a withdrawal from life. "Sitting Bull used a dream-vision to short-circuit reality rather than to engage with it" (Lear 2008: 150). When a ritual takes over one's entire life, this is a faulty form of life—in this case it can be seen as an avoidance of the difficult choices, the unpleasant compromises and hard work, which the situation required (Lear 2008: 151). Furthermore, letting a ritual become the meaning of one's life can be seen as an attempt of controlling life, of creating security and certainty in the face of the unavoidable vulnerability and uncertainty that any human life entails, but especially so during times of war and colonisation. What the Sioux accomplished through their dance was not control and security, only the temporary illusion of it, something which like a drug could fend off despair for a short period of time, but not solve the extensive political and existential problems they were facing. So even though the attempt of magically controlling life given the circumstances is understandable, it is nevertheless not a humanly excellent response to it.

> One needs to recognize the destruction that has occurred if one is to move beyond it. [...] It is one thing to dance as though nothing has happened; it is another to acknowledge that something singularly awful has happened [...] and then decide to dance. (Lear 2008: 152, 153)

Plenty Coups' vision, on the other hand, was interpreted and put to use in a way that allowed the Crow to face total destruction and respond well to the reality of that. It "gave them an ideal in relation to which they could aim for something fine", namely to hold on to their land and work for a transformation of the Crow form of life. It further did so in a way that allowed them to take actual practical steps to better their lot (Lear 2008: 145, 135–136).

Wittgenstein argued that even if the world changes radically, we can hold on to what is fundamental in our form of life. But he does not stop his investigation at this point. He goes on to show that our ability to 'stay in the saddle', despite radical changes in nature, does have its limits. If the Bosch-world turned out to be permanent, it is hard to see how language and practices could stay the same as previously, no matter how hard we would hold on to them (Wittgenstein 2016: § 617). Here is a minor example: "Even if an irregularity in natural events did suddenly occur, that wouldn't *have* to throw me out of the saddle. I might make inferences then just as before, but whether one would call that ‚induction' is another question" (Wittgenstein 2016: § 619). Our concept of 'induction' is connected with the possibility of observance of regularities in nature. If such regularities disappear, then we cannot do the same thing, as we did before under the name of 'induction'. We might keep the name, but it would be a different concept, that is, in this case part of our justification-practice *would* change, as observing regularities in the past is what we now considered a good reason for expecting it to happen in the future (Wittgenstein 2009: § 480–486; Hodges 1995: 103).

> The more abnormal the case, the more doubtful it becomes what we are to say. And if things were quite different from what they actually are—if there were, for instance, no characteristic expression of pain, of fear, of joy; if rule became exception, and exception rule; or if both became phenomena of roughly equal frequency—our normal language-games would thereby lose their point. (Wittgenstein 2009: § 142)

If the Bosch-world, with its evaporating houses, its talking cows, and its human-tree-transformations, became permanent, this would be an example of a world, where what is now an exception becomes the rule, and where large parts of our current 'knowledge-and justification-language-games' would lose their point. How would our practices develop, if nature changed like that? What would it mean to be justified in claiming to have knowledge of the world in this world? Despite being linguistically well-formed, the questions nonetheless seem to lack a clear meaning. The Bosch-world is a case, where it is 'doubtful what we are to say', as the example is extremely bizarre. Would we stop using wood for fire and furniture, because trees sometimes turn into humans and vice versa? Probably. But if this really happened, our whole worldview, our entire understanding of physics and biology, of what it means to be a human being, what to trust and what not to trust and numerous other things would change. There is no way of predicting what our life form and practices would evolve into—or if we would even be able to survive at all. The Sioux could thus choose to 'stay in the saddle' and hold on to their old way of life. But they could not choose that doing so amounted to living well. Nussbaum remarks: Within different spheres of existence, we often have to ask ourselves "what is it to choose and respond well within that sphere [of existence]? And what is it to choose defectively?" (Nussbaum 2002: 245). Even in extreme conditions, like the one the Crow and Sioux were facing, life thus still faces humans with a challenge not only to live but also to live well.

When debating the possibility of comparison of forms of life, it can be useful to distinguish between two kinds of cases. One, where the question of the right standards for comparing the quality of different forms of life as well as determining the fact of the matter is very complex, debatable and even unanswerable, because we, for instance, lack access to the empirical sources, but where there in principle is an answer to be known. Another case, where the question is meaningless, because it is 'malformed' and involves a misuse of concepts (Brandhorst 2015: 230; Wittgenstein 2009: § 47; Kuusela 2008: 139). Here there is no answer, and thus no right answers, to be known—like there is no answer to the question 'What is the highest: these baby-screams, the Eiffel tower or that junkie over there?'[6] The general question 'Which form of life, the Crow before 1800 or a modern life, is the better?' seems to fall in the latter category rather than the former. However, if the question asked was a lot more specific—like 'Given the criteria WHO use to determine how children thrive, which of the two forms of life was best for children age 5–7?'—it could fall in the former category.

When discussing moral change, one difficult balancing act is between on the one hand paying justice to 'the fact of change' (to differences and to different concepts, practices and forms of life) and on the other hand paying justice to 'the fact of permanence' (to overlaps and likenesses between concepts, practices and forms of life). In Moody-Adams' attempt to bring out and underline the aspects of continuity and likenesses between different historical epochs end cultures, she seems to go too far and ends up neglecting the differences (which the thinkers, she criticises, do seem to overestimate). Overlaps are needed in order to compare concepts, values and forms of life, but not something which "*strongly* resembles one's own familiar set of beliefs". The Crow-story displays some of the complexity in changes of a whole form of life and discussions of comparison and evaluation: How there, for instance, can be both ethically incommensurable traits, but also aspects, which are comparable before and after the change. What is 'different' and 'common' between two cultures, and even between two humans, is often such a complicated crisscross of varying differences and likenesses. Like plants, humans flourish in many ways.

[6] I believe this way of illustrating a meaningless question, just with different questions, stems from Peter Hacker's work, but I have not been able to locate the reference. I know for certain to have also learned it from the engaging lectures by Jørgen Husted.

CHAPTER 17

# Moral Progress

> There has been no moral counterpart to material progress. (Posner 1998a: 1679)

In the Introduction to this part of the book, Moody-Adams expressed the view that humans need to believe in moral progress (Moody-Adams 2017: 153). "Moral progress implies, in the first instance, a change in circumstances for the better." (Wilson 2010: 97). If a thinker claims that there can be moral progress, then this entails the claim that we can evaluate changes ethically (Rønnow-Rasmussen 2017: 137). Moral progress is thus an ethically positively evaluated change.[1] If we evaluate changes ethically, we do so according to certain measuring-rods like ideals, ideas, values, aims or criteria. Believing in the possibility of 'moral progress' also entails accepting the possibility of 'moral decline', that is ethically negatively evaluated changes. If things can go 'right', 'be good' and so on and thus live up to the criteria for this, it logically entails the possibility they can also fail and not live up to the ideals and criteria for the morally good (Wittgenstein 2009: §§ 138–242).[2] Our vocabulary contain both words designating a

[1] Musschenga and Meynen (2017) offer an overview of the current dominant understandings of moral progress.

[2] Wittgenstein's views on progress have been discussed by among others von Wright (1994), Read (2016), Hermann (2015), Holt (1997), Morawetz (2000b), Bouveresse (2011), Pleasants (2000), Moore (2010), Cerbone (2003), Hill (1997), Crary (2000a, 2007c), Tully (2003), Diamond (2012, 2016, 2019) and Heyes (2003). Wittgenstein was



C. Eriksen, *Moral Change*,
https://doi.org/10.1007/978-3-030-61037-1_17

negatively evaluated change, like 'regression', 'decline', 'deteriorate', 'decay', 'worsen' and 'corrupt', as well as words for a positively evaluated change, like 'progress', 'reformation', 'uplift', 'restore', 'boost' and 'improvement'. Some words, like 'development', are used both neutrally and positively as in the remarks 'There has been a development in the case' (here we don't know yet if this is good or bad), and 'She has developed tremendously over the last year' (here we would assume it was good).

I believe Moody-Adams is right, that humans need to believe in some form of progress in order to have the courage and stamina to act in a world that give us plenty of reasons to despair. This is the idea of fruitful hope. The hope of actually doing something good, and not only believing to be doing something good. One could live in the latter kind of vain hope due to being naive, to having been politically deceived or having been brainwashed growing up in a religious sect. The possibility of hope and the nature of the criteria and measuring rods we have for evaluating moral change is the topic of this section.

In the aforementioned quote, Posner rejects the idea that there is moral progress in the same sense there has been material and scientific progress.[3] He does not, however, claim that the concept of moral progress lacks sense. The criteria for pronouncing a moral claim like 'the abolition of slavery is moral progress':

> are relative to the moral code of the particular culture in which the claim is advanced, so that we cannot call another culture 'immoral', unless we add '*by our lights*'. [...] the morality that condemns the traitor or the adulterer cannot itself be evaluated in moral terms; that would be possible only if there were reasonably concrete transcultural moral truths. (Posner 1998a: 1642, 1643, my italics)

Moral ideals, values, criteria and so forth are only locally binding. They are only ethically valid internally in a society and culture and thus not trans-historically or trans-culturally. According to Posner, a person, practice or society can be morally evaluated relative to the societies' own moral goals

sceptical about what he saw as his time's blind faith in the idea of progress; especially the hopes for what scientific and technological progress could accomplish. Yet, he was not a conservative thinker (Diamond 2016; Crary 2000a, 2007c; Heyes 2003: 4–9).

[3] Initially, Posner did claim that "that no useful meaning can be given to the expression 'moral progress' and that no such progress can be demonstrated" (Posner 1998a: 1641). This, as we will see further, was later modified.

(Posner 1998b: 1813–1814). We can, therefore, talk about moral progress when a society progresses according to its own moral ideals and values. "To us, slavery is an abomination, so we consider its abolition a mark of moral progress" (Posner 1998b: 1815). We can also know moral truth—like the fact in Posner's society infanticide is, in most circumstances, considered immoral. However, we cannot say that slavery or infanticide is immoral *as such*, independent of what a particular local community holds to be true. Therefore, an outsider to a culture can criticise the moral code of that culture—but it is according to criteria valid only in this person's own culture (Posner 1998a: 1645). My critique offers no moral reasons to and has no moral hold on the slave owners.

Posner is here offering what we can call 'a community view of moral normativity':[4] the idea that the agreement of the community determines the meaning of words, like the meaning of moral progress/decline, right/wrong, just/unjust, courageous/cowardly and so forth. In the following, the focus will be on the term 'moral progress'. The 'community conception' of normativity comes in two versions, and both will be discussed next: one is that 'moral progress' means what the community has *agreed upon* calling 'moral progress'—for instance, through forms of dialogue in ideal speech situations or through democratic majority rule. The other is to take community agreement as involving no active action on behalf of the community (no interpretation, no agreeing, no decision, no voting, etc.). Here agreement means not coming to an agreement but *being in* agreement—as a matter of regularity due to, for example, a common biology or as a matter of alike enculturation and upbringing. According to this interpretation 'moral progress' means what the majority of people as a matter of their natural or culturally determined attunement considers moral progress in this society.

Rorty agrees with Posner that there cannot be formulated any objective moral "criteria of choice between final vocabularies", that is, between "a culture's conceptual framework", "a historical epoch" or a "worldview" (Rorty 1989: 73, 75; 2007: 917, 925; 1999: xv). But he nonetheless argues that we ethically legitimately can evaluate, for example, norms and

[4] However, Posner is somewhat difficult to interpret in this regard, as he also seems to *reject* such an interpretation of his thinking (see, e.g. Posner 1998a: 1705; 1998b). However, Nussbaum, Moody-Adams and Rønnov-Rasmussen, among others, also interpret him along the same lines as I will do here.

practices across time and between cultures (Rorty 2007; Moody-Adams 2017: 168). Rorty morally confidently declares:

> I think that our norms are better than those of our ancestors. [...] We in the modern West know much more about right and wrong than we did two centuries ago, just as we know much more about how nature works. We have been equally successful in both morals and physics. (Rorty 2007: 918, 921)

An example of this progress, which Rorty offers us, is that 'we and our judges' (i.e. Americans in 2007), unlike those who drafted the Eight Amendment, find the use of lash and stocks as punishment of criminals cruel and have therefore changed the practice of criminal punishment (Rorty 2007: 922). "Moral progress is a matter of wider and wider sympathy" (Rorty 1999: 82), and the criteria of 'wide sympathy' can be applied to other cultures than Rorty's own. Rorty concedes that the moral standards we use to evaluate changes are local and may change themselves, yet we can still asses moral progress.[5] He is not, however, claiming, like Posner would say, that we are morally better 'by our light'. We are morally better 'period'. In the same way Rorty is also not claiming, we are medically better at curing broken limps and infectious diseases now than 700 years ago 'by our light', but medically better at this 'period'. Truth is not, like hot and high, a relative term: "Eternal and absolute truth is the only kind of truth there is" (Rorty 2007: 923, see also Rorty 1989: 84; 2007: 922, 925). It is true that uses of the lash is a cruel punishment today, as it was 200 years ago.

When Rorty, and many other philosophers, refuses to accept 'moral progress' equals 'moral progress by our light', I believe this is best understood as what Wittgenstein calls 'a grammatical remark'; that is a remark on the meaning of the word in question—here the concept of moral progress. Even though human agreement and attunement are very significant

[5] Rorty is therefore a representative of what Roth calls 'a non-utopian view of moral progress' (Roth 2012: 385, 389), which means he does not assume any fixed 'higher order' moral standards to evaluate changes, as 'utopian conceptions of moral progress' do. Wilson also argues "that we can acknowledge the existence of moral truths and moral progress without being committed to moral realism" (Wilson 2010: 97), and further claims that "moral belief change for the better shares certain features with theoretical progress in the natural sciences" (Ibid.). Raz is an example of a modern utopian—arguing that we need unchanging moral principles in order to explain and assess changes in moral thinking (Raz 1994).

phenomenon for the ethical life of humans, their role is not that they determine what moral progress—or any other word used with a moral aim—amounts to; they do not enter morality *that* way.[6]

To see that they are not doing so, we can start by reminding ourselves how questions of moral evaluation are dealt with in everyday life. When we try to find out what would be a morally good way forward (or mean and cruel, we do that too) in a given situation, we do not call PricewaterhouseCoopers, ask them to conduct a survey in our society to find the answer and then consider the survey-result the final say in the matter. We also do not conduct a vote and think that the moral matter is finally settled with that. Nor do we consult an anthropological work on the morality of the Swedes and let that decide the question for us. "An ethical sentence says 'You must do that!' or 'This is good!' but not 'People say that this is good'" (Wittgenstein in Christensen 2011: 812). In other words, we do not use the term 'moral progress' equivalently with the expression 'what most people in a society say is or can agree on or are attuned to see as moral progress'. The meanings of the terms are different, and we have different methods and criteria for establishing what is moral progress and for what people in a society treat or can agree on as moral progress. Therefore, the former cannot be reduced to a matter of any of the latter. "From its *seeming* to me—or to everyone—to be so, it doesn't follow that it *is* so" (Wittgenstein 2016: § 2)—a conceptual fact, which is the mother of many Greek tragedies and tragic societies. Even if all members of the Peoples Temple in Jonestown considered it a good thing to commit collective suicide, it makes sense to disagree and argue they were morally wrong. This would not, as a matter of logic, be the case if 'being morally right' conceptually amounted to 'being morally right by a society's light'. The politicians of Sweden in 1902 thought they were creating moral progress by helping criminal, neglected and orphaned children getting better lives with their new childcare laws. However, they were mistaken. In other words: "It is up to us what we do. But it is never up to us, whether what we cause, by doing so, is good or bad" (Fink 2010: 311, my translation). This is a matter of 'the grammar of the ethical'—of how we use our words

[6]By means of criticising both versions of 'the community view of normativity', Wittgenstein's work is inspirational. See, for example Wittgenstein 2009: §§ 241–242; 2001: Part 3 § 65–67, Part 6 § 30, Part 7 § 40; 2004: §§ 429–431; 2016: § 2. Williams 2009: 18; Hacker 1972: 298. For similar argumentative strategies against moral relativism, see, for example Lear 1984 and Jaeggi 2018.

when using them with an ethical point. 'Moral progress' cannot be defined as that which a society considers or agrees on is moral progress. Moral mistakes, wrongdoing and decline is a possibility not only in an individual level, but also on the levels of a practice or a society.

However, all of the above—votes, dialogues, human attunement, anthropological knowledge of what people considers good and bad, and so forth—*can* enter as morally relevant things to consider in our attempt to figure out what moral progress would be in a particular case. For example, attunement is an important trait for and of our practices with words like 'cruel' or 'morally bad' and for the human rights' legal practices. Here it matters that there is a human attunement in the consequences of, for example, sleep and food depravation and use of isolation—the fact that we can predict that humans will not thrive without sleep, food and company. The role of the human attunement in our practices is part of what makes them possible, as investigated in the previous section—it works as a fundamental condition for them, and it can also constitute part of their character (Wittgenstein 2004: § 430; Williams 2009: 9–12). If not votes, attunement or consensus reach by dialogue settle for us what moral progress is, what then does?

Nothing, if what is asked for are criteria valid across all the possible situations, we might evaluate (Diamond 2012: 197). When looking back at the narratives in Part 1, we can see that the transformation of the practice of feuds into a legal compensations-system in societies in Europe and Scandinavia in the Middle Ages was hailed as moral progress, and the reasons for this is that it spared the families of sorrow and the lives of many men, now able to work and bring greater prosper to their families and villages. In the 1700–1900s the industrialised countries of Europe passed new laws on child labour and found ways of effectuating them so no child should work in a chimney and get 'inflammations of the eye-lids, bruises, burns, and stunted growth and deformity of the spine, legs and arms because of the long periods of time in abnormal positions'. These laws have been regarded as a morally good development, because they put an end to suffering and exploitation of children. The de-criminalisation and later legal equality for homosexuals in Denmark and the rest of Europe has been seen as moral progress due to the end of unfair discrimination and because it allowed homosexuals—as well as their families—to live with less fear of negative social stigmatisation, of pathologisation and of legal prosecution. It allowed them to live openly with their partners and children, and so forth. In other words, a development is deemed progress on the background of a variety of different criteria and parameters. Which criteria and ideals are relevant to use depends on the case and context at hand, something which will be further elaborated in the concluding sections of this book.

Posner claimed that 'moral intuitions don't link up with anything outside us, you cannot tell me to look harder, you cannot show me that my intuition is an illusion, there are no crucial experiments, by which we can validate a moral argument, there are no morally reputable persons, no useful inventions embodying moral theory, and no moral counterpart to material progress' (Posner 1998a: 1679). I have argued that moral intuitions can link up with things outside us. My moral intuition could have been that single parenting was not necessarily harmful for children. When Western societies and social moralities changed, so that single mothers and fathers and their children were no longer automatically socially stigmatised and morally condemned by the rest of society (bastards!), it turned out that my intuition was confirmed (see, e.g. Baker 2019: 27–35). The opposite happens as well.

In other words: You can thus tell me to look harder, I can do so, and as a result see morally better—like Zaal, the neo-Nazi, who through becoming a father acquired a new view of his beliefs and political ideology and as a result revised them. You can show me, or I can discover that my moral intuition is an illusion, like the women's movement have shown that what many of us thought was just 'compliments' and 'good office fun' were in fact unpleasant and degrading treatment of our female fellow co-workers. There are indeed people, who are 'morally reputable', who can help us, through company, conversations and by been ethical examples. Of those people we can think 'what would Malala or Mandala have done here?' and to remember the life of these humans can sometimes illuminate the darkness and lift the fear or confusion we are in. There are also crucial experiments, big and small, by which we can validate a moral argument. What we understand as cruel treatment of people in prison—like extensive use of isolation—stems from having tried out different forms of punishment in various prison camps around the world (Guenther 2013). This has given us information, which we can use to validate our arguments. And there are what can be called moral inventions helping people live better lives—for instance, the invention of a compensation system instead of vendettas—which constitute moral progress. Human life is filled with exactly those things, giving us reasons not to despair and have hope.

CHAPTER 18

# Conclusion: Contextual Ethics

> Let us now consider what we can do if a patient asks what the meaning of his life *is*. [...] I doubt whether a doctor can answer this question in general terms. For the meaning of life differs from man to man, from day to day and from hour to hour. [...] Ultimately, man should not ask what the meaning of his life is, but rather he must recognize that it is *he* who is asked. In a word, each man is questioned by life. (Frankl 2004: 113)

At the end of Part I, we found ourselves entangled in a Gordian knot: The fact of moral change seemed to undermine our ability to judge and act ethically legitimately, while at the same time life relentlessly raises ethical demands to us that we must judge and act. The way out of the knot was to look at the threads one by one and dissolve them by showing that the moral sceptical doubts, which lead us into the knot, lack sense. For that reason, they are incapable of challenging our moral values, concepts, ideals and practices, and were rejected. In this way released from the Gordian knot, we were set free to judge and act—only to encounter ethical worries and challenges, which cannot be dismissed: When we disagree morally, how should we as individuals, as groups and our political and legal system best handle that? How can we ensure our schools, workplaces, living areas, food production, political, legal and health system support good lives, when the world or fundamental parts of morality changes?

Faced with the fluidity of morality, philosophers also concerned have asked 'If the idea of an Archimedean vantage point is an empty illusion, how can a form of life be analysed and criticized as unsuccessful or


C. Eriksen, *Moral Change*,
https://doi.org/10.1007/978-3-030-61037-1_18

damaged? What are the sources of ethical normativity?' The answer to these latter questions worked out in this book is that a form of life can merit ethical critique in multiple ways. It can, for instance, be criticised as unsuccessful if it does not take care of basic human needs and vulnerabilities. If it does not provide us with something fine to live up to. If it creates suffering and blocks for human flourishing. The sources of ethical critique—and creativity—we encountered in the narratives and discussions of this book were dialogue, language, human biology, ethical ideals and values, art, myths, experiences, history, religion and religious faith, literature, dreams, practical judgement, suffering, visions, love, ironic disruption, poetry, culture meetings, intuition and international laws. All of this, and countless other things, can be sources of ethical critique and creativity.

There is not one primary, fundamental or privileged source of ethical normativity. Further, the list is necessarily open-ended. What is a reason for ethical critique, or a fruitful source of ethical creativity depends entirely on the situation and context at hand—on what ethical tasks we are facing. What is a good ethical inspiration for how to transform the future of a whole society in one context—like a nine-year-old's vision was for the Crow—could in another context be a deluded, if not insane strategy. That we all need food and shelter is universally true of human life, but it is not always the ethically most relevant trait of a situation. In Ibsen's play *A Doll's House*, Nora's husband could have said to her 'But I provide a roof over your head and plenty of food, so why do you want to leave?!', and that would amount to being blind to what was ethically at stake in Nora's life at that point. As it was the cases with the investigation in Part I of the dynamics of moral change, a similar complex and at times holistic picture emerges from the investigation in Part II. Though it makes sense to claim that the ethical normativity in some situations stems from a certain, distinguishable source (that for instance the reason why starvation is harmful stems from human biology), then the ethical normativity can also be emanating from the situation as a whole. The account of the normativity of moral change given in this part of the book can therefore be characterised as *pluralistic*, *holistic* and *contextual.*

Such conception of ethical normativity allows for the existence of different forms of life, which nevertheless—because of phenomena like common traits in the human form of life, overlaps in human languages and cultural complexity—does not preclude the possibility of moral dialogue and legitimate ethical critique of those forms of life. Therefore, this conception of ethical normativity creates space for cultural and moral pluralism without sliding into a cynical, laissez-faire subjectivism and allows for ethical critique without sliding into dogmatic fundamentalism. It enables what Moody-Adams terms 'moral confidence': "the possibility of engaging in non-coercive action in a culturally complex world: that condition might be called moral confidence: confidence both in the making of moral judgements that purport to apply, legitimately, across cultures, and in the worth of trying to convince others of their legitimacy" (Moody-Adams 2002: 23).

One central question, raised in the introduction, has not yet been answered, namely: What *is* 'the ethical'? *What* changes in moral changes, as opposed to, for example, aesthetic, social or political changes? Throughout the investigations and discussions of this book, it has to some extent remained an open question what the 'moral' in moral changes is. In these concluding sections, I will argue why it necessarily has to remain so, while at the same time unfolding a conceptualisation of the ethical termed 'contextual ethics'.

But before I answer the aforementioned questions, I first need to say a few words on the status of such an answer. In 1934 Wittgenstein notes, "If we look at the actual use of a word, what we see is something constantly fluctuating." He continues with the following remarks on his philosophical method:

> In our investigations we set over against this fluctuation something more fixed, just as one paints a stationary picture of a constantly altering landscape. When we study language we *envisage* it as a game with fixed rules. We compare it with, and measure it against, a game of that kind. [...]. Thus it could be said that the use of the word 'good' (in an ethical sense) is a combination of a very large number of interrelated games, each of them, as it were a facet of the use. (Wittgenstein, in Kuusela 2008: 142)

This quote provides a useful image or frame for how to understand 'the ethical' in human life as well as for understanding the activity and history of moral philosophy. The ethical can be pictured as something with different *facets*, which consists of 'a very large number of interrelated games' (see also Wittgenstein 2009: § 75–77). The claim here is thus not that the ethical *is* something that consists of a large number of language-games.[1] The claim is it can—for certain purposes—be a useful image to understand the ethical through. It casts a light on aspects of the ethical, which are important when seeking to understand moral change (but it might not be helpful for other kinds of philosophical investigations; that is left an open question; see also Wittgenstein 2009: §§130–133). Another way of getting at this is to say that the status of the following conceptualisation of ethics is to be understood as an 'ideal type' or '*Gedankenbild*'.[2]

In order to address the issue of how to understand the moral in moral change, I will in the following sections sum up the remarks on the nature of morality found in Parts I and II and elaborate a conception of the ethical along four irreducible dimensions, namely the transcendental, the immanent, the absolute and the transcending.[3]

## The Ethical as Transcendental

Over time and across cultures, anthropologists have found that the ethical in a broad sense is a universal aspect of human life (Keane 2016a: 6):

> Ethnographers commonly find that the people they encounter are trying to do what they consider right or good, are being evaluated according to criteria of what is right and good, or are in some debate about what constitutes the human good. (Lambek 2010: 1)

'The ethical' and 'the human' can, however, be said to be even more intimately related, than what a general empirical correlation between humans and morality entail. The following quote gives a hit to how:

[1] Here my moral philosophical use of Wittgenstein's concept of language-games differs from Pleasants' (2008) and Hermann's (2015).

[2] 'Ideal type' and '*Gedankenbild*' are terms borrowed from Weber (Weber 2009: 25–26, 42, 63, 132). Kuusela unfolds it like this: "[An ideal type] is used to draw attention to certain characteristics of the objects of investigation, but to what extent the latter actually correspond to the former is left open. […] the model becomes 'a picture with which we compare reality, through which we represent how things are; […] where 'reality' includes anything one might want to take as one's object of investigation" (Kuusela 2008: 125).

[3] The idea of having several irreducible dimensions of a concept stems from Hyman's treatment of the concept of human agency (Hyman 2015: iv). In unfolding a contextual understanding of ethics, I am inspired by the work of Wittgenstein, Løgstrup, Diamond, Fink and Crary (see, e.g. Eriksen forthcoming).

> The point here is not that people are necessarily motivated to be good (rather than, say, malicious or cruel) or that they are never misled by violent or callous ideologies. Rather, the cultural point is that moral striving seems to matter a great deal to people in all sorts of societies. What constitutes the good life may vary widely from society to society, but it is difficult to imagine any community where this does not matter or where, if it has ceased to be important, this does not seem problematic for its members. (Mattingly 2014: 11)

What Mattingly points to this quote with the remark 'it is difficult to imagine' is that not only is the presence of 'the ethical' in some form an universal empirical fact about the human form of life, which can be validated though anthropological, sociological, historical, psychological and archaeological research into past and present human life. The ethical can also be said to characterise the human condition in a stronger and more fundamental sense, namely as what we can call 'a transcendental condition' for human life.[4]

This means that the concept of 'a human being' is the concept of a creature living an ethical form of life and inhabiting an ethically structured world. A lifeworld not structured that way would not be recognisable as a human world.[5] It should, therefore, come as no surprise that when we empirically investigate the past and other cultures in the present, all these different cultures display some form of morality. If we came across a creature physically identical to humans, yet their lives would not display anything we could term 'moral', then we would deem these creatures not humans (like the creatures in the horror movie *Invasion of the Body Snatchers*). If we can call something 'a human being' or 'a human society', it follows that ethical issues are at stake in various ways with this being and

[4] The use of this term here differs from (some interpretations of) Kant's use of the term in at least two crucial ways: First, the transcendental here is not to be understood as conditioned by 'the human mind's setup'. No form of idealism is implied. 'The ethical is a transcendental condition for human life' is in Wittgenstein's sense 'a grammatical remark'; a remark about our practice with the word 'human'. The other way it differs from (some interpretations of) Kant is that he seems to understand the transcendental as unchanging. The concept of human life has always been an ethical life, as far as we can tell. But concepts do change, and the ethical can thus *in principle* cease having the role of transcendental condition for human life. Yet, currently, this possibility lacks sense.

[5] Christensen unfolds a reading of Wittgenstein's conception of ethics, early and late, similar to this idea (Christensen 2003, 2011). Wittgenstein characterises both logic and the ethical as transcendental because they "structure reality" (Christensen 2003: 132).

society. Therefore, it is not a psychological matter about our imagination or lack of it, that we 'cannot imagine' a non-moral human life.

Being human means that one is not only faced with a need for food, company and sleep, but also faced with an ethical challenge of living a good life. Ethical normativity is not something that is 'added on to' or 'developed out of' a biological or purely physical concept of human nature: "being human involves [...] living up to an ideal. Being human is thus linked to a conception of human excellence" (Lear 2011: 3). This aspect of human nature can serve as a measuring rod for ethical evaluation of changes in individuals, practices and forms of life. To describe the ethical as a transcendental condition for human life is to invoke a very thin understanding of the ethical, and it does not really answer what kind of changes we are looking at when investigating moral changes. The next section will therefore further unfold how the ethical can be characterised.

## The Ethical as Absolute

> Supposing that I could play tennis and one of you saw me playing and said 'Well, you play pretty badly' and suppose I answered 'I know, I'm playing badly but I don't want to play any better,' all the other man could say would be 'Ah then that's all right.' But suppose I had told one of you a preposterous lie and he came up to me and said 'You're behaving like a beast' and then I were to say 'I know I behave badly, but then I don't want to behave any better,' could he then say 'Ah, that's all right'? Certainly not; he would say 'Well, you *ought* to want to behave better.' Here you have an absolute judgment of value. (Wittgenstein 1993a: 38–39)

Wittgenstein here points to 'the ethical' as an *absolute* measuring rod for human behaviour, which means that it applies to us whether we as individuals or as a group accept or are aware of it or not (Fink 2010: 310, 317). Other terms for this aspect of the ethical could be, for example, 'radical', 'unconditional', 'infinite', 'universal' or 'timeless' (Fink 2007: 318). Yet, it is crucial that these words, like the equally philosophically charged word 'transcendental', point to *the role* that the ethically good play in our lives. In this section as a demand humans no matter what ought to try to live up to (except in border cases like infants, people in coma or severely mentally ill). It does not amount to for instance an empirical claim about time—about how *long* the ethical will be around (for ever). Løgstrup unfolds a similar line of thinking:

> it is not at our discretion whether we want to live in relationships of responsibility or not, but the individual finds themselves in them just by existing. They are always already responsible, whether they want to be or not, because they have not ordered their lives by themselves. We are born into a life of a very particular order, and this order lays claim on us in such manner that as we grow up, we find ourselves bound to other human beings and forced into the lives of others in relationships of responsibility. (Løgstrup 2020: 91–92)

Human beings are creatures with a free will. It is up to us whether we want to ignore or try to live up to what life ethically asks of us. Yet, when doing so, it is never up to us, whether *what* we cause is ethically good or bad (Fink 2010: 311). It is, for instance, not our good or bad intentions, whether we acted willingly or unwillingly, knowingly or unknowingly, that determine, if what our action accomplished was good or bad. That is beyond our will, reach and power.

> The demand of the situation is that I do not let the other down. Not to conceive this as a demand is to not care whether 'life shall flourish or be destroyed'. One can do that; but it cannot be good to do that. (Fink 2010: 311, my translation)

As a matter of how we use the words good and evil, when we use them with an ethical aim, it is 'not up to us to decide, whether it is better to do good than to do evil' (Fink 2007: 52, my translation). We can choose to disregard what a situation ethically demands of us, but we cannot do so without failing and being blameworthy (Løgstrup 2020). The ethical is what in an absolute sense ought to matter to me, to you and to us.

Where this section stressed the given, universal and absolute aspect of the ethical, the next section will focus on the immanent, particular and contextual aspects.

## The Ethical as Immanent

The ethical is an immanent feature of human life. It unfolds in our dealings with each other and ourselves on a quotidian basis (Lambek 2010: 1–2). This, among many other things, means that acting in ethically good ways comes natural to us. Often, when we see someone stumble and get badly hurt, we spontaneously help without thinking further about whether or how to do it, we run to them, we help them up, we tend to their wounds and we try to stop the bleeding. But acting good is not the only thing that comes naturally to us—we are prone to acting unkind and cruel as well. We know from ourselves, from our family and neighbours, from what history has taught us, about the unsettling human tendencies that lead to violence, to slander, to rape, to using other people as scapegoats or slaves (Wittgenstein 1993b: 143–155; Eriksen 2006: 95–98). Acting good as well as bad can thus be seen as a natural, immanent part of human life just like sleeping, eating and telling stories is.

It is also part of ordinary human upbringing and culture that we are taught about 'the ethical'. As children we are taught and also pick up 'how to behave' in our family and culture. We implicitly and explicitly learn the ethical use of words, including the words we often use with an ethical point, like 'good', 'bad', 'vice', 'virtue', 'coward' and 'brave'. We thus also learn which situations they are used in (Hanfling 2003: 78; Moody-Adams 1999: 18). Normal adults in this sense know and are familiar with what 'the ethical' is. Some of this knowledge can be seen as analogous to knowing that all bachelors are unmarried men (Hanfling 2003). This knowledge entails that we, for instance, know that it is always better to do good than to cause harm, be just than unjust, be brave than a coward, be caring than reckless (Fink 2007: 52).

As mature language users we can recognise the following broad philosophical definitions of ethics as all of them concerning what is called 'the ethical': "'Ethics is the general inquiry into what is good' […] Ethics is the enquiry into what is valuable, or, into what is really important, or […] Ethics is the enquiry into the meaning of life, or into what makes life worth living, or into the right way of living" (Wittgenstein 1993a: 38). "Ethics deals with that we ought to abide by in our lives with each other, but it is not self-evident, what it is we ought to abide by" (Fink 2012: 15, my translation). Human life poses an ethical task to the one living it, namely, to live "a 'life worth living', or a 'good life'" (Mattingly 2014: 9; Lear 2008: 145, 135–136). As long as these broad remarks are not turned into philosophical theories, they represent fairly uncontroversial ways of loosely elaborating some of what 'the ethical' is about, which catches central ethical concerns recognisable from many human cultures.

But what we learn as children, when learning what 'the ethical' is, is far from reducible to intellectually knowing how to use words in a correct way. What we learn is essentially ***a doing***. To master the concept of 'justice' entails acting in just ways, not only being able to form a meaningful sentence with the word in it. In ethical upbringing we learn to notice certain aspects of the world from an early age, we learn how to act on them, and how we *ought* to act on them (Aristotle 1976: 95; Hanfling 2003: 30–32). In Aristotle's words:

> [Eudaimonia] is acquired by moral goodness and by some kind of study or training [...] Moral goodness [...] is the result of habit [...] we become just by performing just acts, temperate by performing temperate ones, brave by performing brave ones. (Aristotle 1976: 80, 91–92)

As adults most of us thus have an intimate grasp of what 'the ethical' is, how to act ethically well and not so well and how to think, evaluate, justify and criticise from an ethical perspective.

The immanence of the ethical also entails that the ethical good and bad is contextually determined (Aristotle 1976: 96). What is ethically demanded of us, and what 'a worthy life' consists in, depends on the context, which a life is shaped by and in which it unfolds. Among other things it depends on what country, what social class, what family one is born into, and what kind of person one is:

> In other words, the [ethical] demand is, as it were, refracted through a prism in a variety of ways. In the first place are the various distinctive relationships in which we stand to one another—as spouses, parents and children, employer and employee, teacher and student, and so on. The demand is refracted through the spiritual content of these relationships, and since this is different from one people to another, from one time to another, the refraction takes place in a great variety of ways. Care of a spouse's life involves different conduct under monogamy than polygamy, just as care for the life of a child required different actions in a patriarchal family and social structure than in family and social life today. (Løgstrup 2020: 91)

Even though it stands fast for every normal adult that 'it is better to do good than bad', and even though 'doing good' often comes naturally to us, then because of the importance of the context and the specific situation, it often requires a lot more than this to know and do the ethically required. We cannot meaningfully debate if it is better to do bad than good. But we can, do and must often reflect on, seek knowledge and debate whether this, perhaps what we in this family calls good, really is an instance of something good, and what in this situation would amount to doing the right thing. Here context comes in and plays a decisive role in determining what the good, just, right, courageous, dignified or so forth is.

To conceptualise the ethical as immanent is also to underline that the ethically demanded and thus the upright, noble, loving, decent, generous or just—as well at the corrupt, depraved, cruel, or unscrupulous—can be fully manifests in our lives. It can be incarnated in, for example, a certain action, remark, judgement, gesture, tone of voice or situation. We meet the ethically good in many everyday situations such as the love and care unfolding between parents and children, the courage and skills of certain politicians, the joy, help and support manifested in our friendships or in the kindness of strangers. In these relations and actions there can be a restless fulfilling of what the situation and relation asks of us ethically.

Yet even though ethical issues are more often ordinary than extraordinary, and that there can be a restless fulfilling of what life in a given situation asks of us ethically, then there are also situations where this is not the case. Cases of liminality, uncertainty, unclarity, confusion and doubt. The very possibility of moral change partly rests in the nature of the ethical itself, in its underdetermined, open, creative and critical facets—in other words in its transcending aspect, which is the last of the dimensions of the ethical described here.

## The Ethical as Transcending

'Ethics' has not always existed as a word (Fink 2012, forthcoming). The adjective 'Ethikos' was created by Aristotle around 350 B.C. as a new formation in the Greek language and it appears in his book *The Nicomachean Ethics* (ibid.). It was created from the word *ethos.* "*Ethos* originally signified both individual moral character and community custom" (Wolcher 2012: 534). But even so, as Fink remarks, we can without further ado recognise that people still had moral problems and reflected ethically upon these problems as well as on their lives and societies before they had a word for these sufferings and activities. Plato's dialogues on the nature of justice show us that people reflected on problems of an ethical nature without having a word for the ethical (Fink 2012). A conversation, action, law, situation or novel can thus deal with ethical issues without directly mentioning words like 'good', 'bad', 'just' or 'moral' (Crary 2007b: 311–312). These would be novels, laws and situations that would *warrant* a use of the word 'ethical' to describe part of what is going on, but it would not be necessary—nor necessarily helpful—in order for us to understand the issues. We can even go a step further and say, as Fink does, that "the ethically and morally important can often best be said without talking about ethics and morals" (Fink 2012: 18, my translation). This is because the moral issue often turns too abstract and empty, when talked about in these words, and furthermore such talk also tends to become moralistic.

An example of the ethical excessiveness of 'moral words' can be seen in the children's book *The Lion, the Witch and the Wardrobe* by C. S. Lewis.[6] Here a possible beginning of the 'breaking bad' of one of the main characters, the child Edmund, is described. Young Edmund's first small, yet serious, moral misstep is to agree to bring his siblings to the seductive and dominant White Queen—a stranger, generous with her box of Turkish Delight, whom he just met for the first time.[7] Edmund lets his sensitivity to the situation, his loyalty and care for his family, and his better judgement be overshadowed by his lust for food, flatter and future power. In other words, he acts in a way we would call human, but here not as a praise (hence the need for writing moral educational books on the subject). Had he not let that happen, the Queen's clearly manipulative behaviour in talking to him like below would most likely have been able to raise his suspicion and made him less willing to bring his siblings to her, without knowing more about this adult and her agenda:

> Instead, she said to him: "Son of Adam, I should so much like to see your brother and your two sisters. Will you bring them to see me?" "I'll try," said Edmund, still looking at the empty box. "Because, if you did come again—bringing them with you of course—I'd be able to give you some more Turkish Delight. [...] It's a lovely place. My house," said the Queen. "I am sure you would like it. There are whole rooms filled with Turkish Delight, and what's more, I have no children of my own. I want a nice boy whom I could bring up as Prince and who would be King of Narnia when I am gone. While he was a Prince he would wear a gold crown and eat Turkish Delight all day long; and you are much the cleverest and handsomest young man, I've ever met. I think I would like to make you the Prince—some day, when you bring the others to visit me." [...] "There's nothing special about

[6] Diamond elaborates on Laura Ingall's *The Long Winter* along similar lines (Diamond 1999).

[7] This is, of course, not the first time Edmund does something ethically bad in his life. Most of us do that on a daily basis, and Edmund has never been 'one of God's best children'. Yet what happens here, as I read the story, is the beginning of a shift—he goes from being above average mean to sliding towards developing 'a bad character'.

them," said Edmund, "and, anyway, I could always bring them to you some other time." (Lewis 2003: 25–26)

Despite no mention of words, which we often use with a moral meaning, like 'evil', 'selfish', 'untrustworthy' or 'greedy', the text nonetheless amounts to a moral teaching in the meeting with a bad person and the first steps of becoming a bad person directed at children. It can even be argued that the text passage would be less ethically good at this if these terms would have been directly mentioned, because then the text would become patronising, and less trusting in its reader's judgement. Hunt remarks on the transformative power of novels that "The novel has worked its effect through the process of involvement in the narrative, not through explicit moralizing" (Hunt 2008: 56).[8] But morally explicit language use and even sentimental moralising can be effective, too, when the goal is to change a person or a practice, as the 'sentimental stories' of children working in the industry show (mentioned in Part I).

This fact—the lack of need to use certain words when talking about, dealing with, educating in, reflecting on and understanding ethical matters—indicates that we should not understand the ethical by only focussing on the use of certain words (e.g. bad, good, voluntariness, duty, happiness and utility). Such a focus will make us understand the ethical too narrowly. What determines a word as 'ethical' is the *way* it is used and *the context* it is used in, not its content (Diamond 1996, 1999; Crary 2007a). The moral meaning of anything, any sign, word, gesture, action, law or institution, is also only determined in the context of specific situations, which are part of a larger historical context, also co-determining the meaning.

I further want to argue that it a bad idea to reduce the ethically essential to 'a certain group of actions' or certain 'language-games/practices' (like care-taking, truth telling, just-dealings, trust, fair-play, promise keeping, reverence), or to delimit it by demanding the presence of 'certain motives' or 'particular causes' for acting (like respect for the moral law, will to power, love of my neighbour, selfish genes, to take care of the other for the sake of the other, neuro-activity in a certain part of the brain). Neither is it fruitful to understand the just only as the results of 'a certain

[8] This is in some respects similar to the method Kierkegaaard employs in his choice of writing pseudonymous works ('indirect communication'), though not in all, as Kierkegaard has a religious aim with his work, namely to help his reader become a true Christian.

procedure' (like reflective equilibrium, 'a rule of action or choice is justified, and thus valid, only if all those affected by the rule or choice could accept it in a reasonable way'). The ethical can also not once and for all be confined and codified by 'laws', 'principles' or 'rules' (like The Ten Commandments, 'the utility principle', 'Act only according to that maxim whereby you can, at the same time, will that it should become a universal law'). To return to Wittgenstein's image, all of these phenomena can be facets of 'the ethical', and they all can be, and often are, morally important.

There is thus nothing wrong in a moral philosopher focussing his or her work on one aspect of what is morally important, like 'taking care' or 'creating a just society'. It all depends on how this is done, what claims are being made and so forth. A good account will yield something truthful about ethics and can give us clarity, help us make better judgements and decisions, and so forth. But no account can 'have the final word'.

> Consequently, there is a tension between knowledge and formulation [of the content and nature of the ethical demand] on the one hand, and the demand and its understanding of life on the other hand. (Løgstrup 2020: 103)

No account can be said to exhaust what there is to say about the ethical, and no aspect in a universal way is the essence or the fundament of 'the ethical'. A certain aspect can be what is central, essential or fundamental for a certain situation, and it can generally be more relevant for a certain area of life than other aspects are. But the ethical can be 'all over the place' (Løgstrup 1995: 8), and "moral thought [...] can in theory range over any subject matter." (Crary 2007b: 313). Furthermore, there is an intrinsic openness or what Lear terms longing to the ethical (Lear 2011):[9] It can transcend 'where' and 'what' it has formerly been.

These remarks do not imply that everything is or will get morally important—for instance, what colour shirt I wear today or how I hold my pencil when writing my shopping list are not morally important. The point is that it can, given the right context, get one. What can become morally important in the future cannot be completely foreseen today. In 1817, I could have a number tattooed on my wrist and a yellow David's star sewed on my jacket, but it would not indicate the same horrible consequences

[9] Vattimo (2005), Lear (2008, 2011) and Waldenfels (2011a, b) each in their way unfold some of what the transcending, openness of the ethical entails.

for my life, as it would, if I were a Jew living in Germany in 1941. The transcending nature of the ethical does also not imply that we should *not* expect that 'taking care of our children' will be as ethically important tomorrow as it is today (and therefore only buy food and diapers for today). But on a less radical scale, new discoveries, technologies, power-shifts, ideals and inventions do change the world, so that things, that were not morally important, become so and vice versa.

Wittgenstein's image of the ethical as something with different facets, which consists of 'a very large number of interrelated games' allows us to think pluralistically, anti-essentialistic and non-reductionistic about ethics—and this way of thinking seems to be rewarding for moral philosophy. This picture allows us to let go of the hunt for what is the true essence of everything we call 'moral' and thus, for instance, avoid the absurd situation of having to choose between, for example, 'consequences', 'obligations' and 'the good life' as the morally more fundamental, as all can be—in some situations and contexts—the ethically salient trait. The picture thus also helps us avoid the choice between the classical moral philosophical theories like the many versions of virtue ethics, consequentialism and deontology. Instead we can see these theories as attempts to capture 'the grammar' (the aim, central values, conceptualisations, principles, logic, etc.) of one of these many interrelated games and thus to elaborate on one facet of the ethical. Moral philosophy can thus be telling us 'the truth', but never 'the whole truth' (Moody-Adams 1999: 169)—and rarely 'nothing but the truth'.

So even though the ethical cannot be finally captured by whatever we, as citizens, legal thinkers, moral philosophers, political and religious visionaries, try to formulate about it, it does not mean that we cannot say any general, accurate and true things about it, neither that there is no point in doing so. Reflecting on and having dialogues about the ethical is an indispensable part of being ethical creatures. For example, creating laws and institutions require us to reflect on and formulate things about what we deem ethically important. Løgstrup expresses this beautifully as we are bound to the norms of our societies in simultaneous distance to them (Løgstrup 2020; see also Lovibond 2019; Delacroix 2017).

A contextual conception of ethics does not preclude that we can talk about universal traits to, for instance, a good human life or that we, like Nussbaum, for political and legal purposes can and in some cases ought to work out lists of, for example, which central capabilities we as a minimum ought to secure, in order for humans everywhere to flourish. However, a contextual ethics does preclude ethical *guarantees*. There is no checklist and no source of normativity, which we can tap into and be assured that we are never morally wrong. We cannot just always check with experience, the ordinary use of the word 'morally good', a universal principle, human nature, our moral intuitions or discuss the matter with the people in the neighbouring nations, and then be assured that our actions, practices, values or form of life are morally good. We can be in the situation that what we are best able to justify morally, nonetheless turns out to be bad (Rorty 1999: 37–39). The ethical authority lies in the situation at hand, not in our ideas or theories about the ethical.

Finally, the transcending dimension of the ethical also shows that no matter how well we have done so far ethically it is in one sense never good enough, namely in the sense that we can never allow ourselves to say 'Now I have done enough morally good for today—and for the rest of my life, for that matter', like we can be justified in saying 'I am done taking piano lessons. I don't want to be better at playing Bach'. Whatever we do, the ethical always demands more of us—it calls for us to move beyond our past good as well as bad deeds.

To conceptualise 'the ethical' as transcendental, absolute, immanent and transcending is not to present a story of something that coherently adds up. It is to accept as inevitable the possibility of dilemmas, conflicts, paradoxes and a need for complementary thinking when it comes to ethics. "But if our life is, ethically speaking, a contradiction, it is important not to remove the contradiction theoretically" (Løgstrup 1997: 167), because we then risk blinding ourselves to what is morally at stake in our lives. Human actions, practices and forms of life can be seen as ongoing moral experiments, conducted in the fleeting as well as more fixed contexts of human life, investigating the question: Will this allow us, our fellow beings, nature and the generations to follow to flourish?

# Bibliography

Alston, P. 2004. 'The Best Interests Principle': Towards A Reconciliation of Culture and Human Rights. In *Children's Rights*, ed. M.D.A. Freeman, vol. 2, 183–208. Hants: Ashgate/Dartmouth.

Andersen, J.G. 2011a. *Borgerne og lovene 2010*. Odense: Syddansk Universitetsforlag.

Andersen, P. 2011b. Klassisk og kristen naturret. In *Retsfilosofi: centrale tekster og temaer*, ed. O. Hammerslev and H. Palmer Olsen, 71–116. Copenhagen: Hans Reitzels Forlag.

Annas, J. 2011. *Intelligent Virtue*. Oxford: Oxford University Press.

Anners, E. 1998. *Den europæiske rettens historie*. Oslo: Universitetsforlaget.

Appiah, K.A. 2010. *The Honor Code: How Moral Revolutions Happen*. New York: W. W. Norton & Company.

Archard, D. 2014. Children's Rights. In *The Stanford Encyclopedia of Philosophy*, ed. E. N. Zalta, Winter 2014 ed. https://plato.stanford.edu/archives/win2018/entries/rights-children/. Accessed 23 June 2017.

———. 2015. *Children: Rights and Childhood*. London: Routledge.

Aristotle. 1976. *Ethics*. London: Penguin Books.

Astma-Allergi Forbundet, et al. 2005. *Passiv Rygning: Hvidbog*. Copenhagen: Dansk Sygeplejeråd. https://www.astma-allergi.dk/documents/10182/11763/Hvidbog-passivrygning.pdf/82b78ad8-511c-455d-8de7-a8b797f05ed2. Accessed 12 June 2017.

Baggini, J., and P.S. Fosl. 2010. *The Philosopher's Toolkit. A Compendium of Philosophical Concepts and Methods*. Malden, MA: Wiley-Blackwell.

Baier, A. 1987. The Need for More than Justice. *Canadian Journal of Philosophy* 17 (13): 41–56.


C. Eriksen, *Moral Change*,
https://doi.org/10.1007/978-3-030-61037-1

Baker, R. 2019. *The Structure of Moral Revolution. Studies of Changes in the Morality of Abortion, Death, and the Bioethics Revolution*. Cambridge, MA: The MIT Press.

Bates, E. 2014. History. In *International Human Rights Law*, ed. D. Moeckli, S. Shah, and S. Sivakumaran. Oxford: Oxford University Press.

Berman, H.J. 1983. *Law and Revolution. The Formation of the Western Legal Tradition*. Cambridge, MA: Harvard University Press.

Bicchieri, C. 2017. *Norms in the Wild. How to Diagnose, Measure, and Change Social Norms*. Oxford: Oxford University Press.

Blake, W. 1926. *Songs of Innocence*. London: Ernest Benn.

Blok, M. 2010. *Niezsche som etiker*. Copenhagen: Museum Tusculanums Forlag.

Bohr, N. 1985. *Naturbeskrivelse og menneskelig erkendelse*. Copenhagen: Rhodos.

Bolinska, A., and J.D. Martin. 2019. Negotiating History: Contingency, Canonicity, and Case Studies. *Studies in History and Philosophy of Science, Part A* 5: 1–24. https://doi.org/10.1016/j.shpsa.2019.05.003.

Bouveresse, J. 2011. Wittgenstein, von Wright and the Myth of Progress. *Paragraph* 34: 301–321.

Brandhorst, M. 2015. Correspondence to Reality in Ethics. *Philosophical Investigations* 38 (3): 227–250.

Brett, R. 2012. Chapter 11: Rights of the Child. In *International Protection of Human Rights: A Textbook*, ed. C. Krause and M. Scheinen. Åbo: Åbo Akademi University.

Brice, R.G. 2013. Mistakes and Mental Disturbance: Pleasants, Wittgenstein, and Basic Moral Certainty. *Philosophia* 41: 477–487.

Bronzo, S. 2012. The Resolute Reading and Its Critics. An Introduction to the Literature. *Wittgenstein-Studien* 3 (1): 45–79.

Buchanan, A., and R. Powell. 2016. Toward a Naturalistic Theory of Moral Progress. *Ethics* 126 (4): 983–1014.

———. 2018. *The Evolution of Moral Progress. A Biocultural Theory*. Oxford: Oxford University Press.

Burian, R.M. 2001. The Dilemma of Case Studies Resolved: The Virtues of Using Case Studies in the History and Philosophy of Science. *Perspectives on Science* 9 (4): 383–404.

Butler, J. 1990. *Gender Trouble*. New York: Routledge.

———. 2002. What Is Critique? An Essay on Foucault's Virtue. In *The Political. Blackwell Readings in Continental Philosophy*, ed. D. Ingram, 212–226. Oxford: Blackwell Publishers.

Cavell, S. 1989. *This Yet Unapproachable America, Lectures after Emerson after Wittgenstein*. Living Batch Press.

———. 1999. *The Claim of Reason: Wittgenstein, Scepticism, Morality and Tragedy*. Oxford University Press.

Cerbone, D.R. 2003. The Limits of Conservatism: Wittgenstein on 'Our Life' and 'Our Concepts'. In *The Grammar of Politics: Wittgenstein and Political Philosophy*, ed. C.J. Heyes, 43–62. New York: Cornell University Press.

Christensen, A.M.S. 2003. Wittgensteins etik. *Slagmark* 38: 125–142.

———. 2011. Wittgenstein and Ethics. In *Oxford Handbook of Wittgenstein*, ed. O. Kuusela and M. McGinn. Oxford: Oxford University Press.

———. 2015. Moral Reasoning & Moral Context: Between Realism and Relativity. In *Realism - Relativism - Constructivism: Contributions of the 38th International Wittgenstein Symposium*, ed. C. Kanzian, J. Mitterer, and K. Neges, 44–46. Frankfurt am Main: Ontos Verlag.

Crary, A. 2000a. Wittgenstein's Philosophy in Relation to Political Thought. In *The New Wittgenstein*, ed. A. Crary and R. Read, 118–146. London: Routledge.

———. 2000b. Introduction. In *The New Wittgenstein*, ed. A. Crary and R. Read, 1–18. London: Routledge.

———. 2007a. Introduction. In *Wittgenstein and the Moral Life*, ed. A. Crary, 1–30. Cambridge, MA: MIT Press.

———. 2007b. Wittgenstein and Ethical Naturalism. In *Wittgenstein and His Interpreters: Essays in Memory of Gordon Baker*, ed. G. Kahane, E. Kanterian, and O. Kuusela. Oxford: Blackwell Publishing.

———. 2007c. Ethics, Inheriting from Wittgenstein. In *Beyond Moral Judgement*, ed. A. Crary, 96–123. Cambridge, MA: Harvard University Press.

Creegan, C.L. 1989. *Wittgenstein and Kierkegaard: Religion, individuality, and philosophical method*. Routledge.

Cunningham, H. 2012. Save the Children, c.1830–c.1920. In *The Global History of Childhood Reader*, ed. H. Morrison, 359–374. Oxon: Routledge.

Daly, C. 2010. *An Introduction to Philosophical Methods*. Ontario: Broadview Press.

De Mesel, B. 2015. Moral Arguments and the Denial of Moral Certainties. In *Realism - Relativism - Constructivism: Contributions of the 38nd International Wittgenstein Symposium*, ed. C. Kanzian, J. Mitterer, and K. Neges, 68–70. Frankfurt am Main: Ontos Verlag.

Del Mar, M. 2011. Introduction. In *New Waves in Philosophy of Law*, ed. M. Del Mar, 1–28. New York: Palgrave Macmillan.

Delacroix, S. 2011. Making Law Bind: Legal Normativity as a Dynamic Concept. In *New Waves in Philosophy of Law*, ed. M. Del Mar, 147–160. New York: Palgrave Macmillan.

———. 2017. Law and Habits. *Oxford Journal of Legal Studies* 37 (3): 660–686.

———. Forthcoming. Standing at Odds with the Usual: Embodied Agency and Triggers for Change. In *Habitual Ethics?* S. Delacroix. London: Hart Publishing. ISBN-13:978-1509920419.

Diamond, C. 1996. Having a Rough Story about What Moral Philosophy Is. In *The Realistic Spirit: Wittgenstein, Philosophy and the Mind*, 13–38. Cambridge, MA: The MIT Press.

———. 1999. Wittgenstein, Mathematics, and Ethics: Resisting the Attractions of Realism. In *The Cambridge Companion to Wittgenstein*, ed. H. Sluga and D.G. Stern, 226–261. Cambridge University Press.

———. 2011. Thoughts about Irony and Identity. In *A Case for Irony*, ed. J. Lear. Harvard University Press.

———. 2012. The Skies of Dante and Our Skies: A Response to Ilham Dilman. *Philosophical Investigations* 35 (3–4): 187–204.

———. 2013. Criticising from Outside. *Philosophical Investigations* 36 (2): 114–132.

———. 2016. Von Wright on Wittgenstein in Relation to His Times. *The 3rd Georg Henrik von Wright Lecture*. Finland: Helsinki University. May. https://www.helsinki.fi/en/projects/the-von-wright-and-wittgenstein-archives/activities/the-georg-henrik-von-wright-lecture#section-85194. Accessed 12 March 2020.

———. 2019. Truth in Ethics: Williams and Wiggins. In *Ethics in the Wake of Wittgenstein*, ed. B. De Mesel and O. Kuusela, 149–179. Oxon: Routledge.

Dübeck, I. 2013. *De elendige. Retshistoriske studier over samfundets marginaliserede*. Copenhagen: Jurist- og Økonomiforbundets Forlag.

Eekelaar, J. 1986. The Emergence of Children's Rights. *Oxford Journal of Legal Studies* 6 (2): 161–182.

Eisele, T.D. 2006. Morawet's 'Roboust Enterprise': Jurisprudence after Wittgenstein. *Philosophical Investigations* 29 (2): 140–179.

Eldridge, R. 2016. *Images of History. Kant, Benjamin, Freedom, and the Human Subject*. Oxford: Oxford University Press.

*Encyclopædia Britannica: Or, A Dictionary of Arts, Sciences, and Miscellaneous Literature* (1910–1922), Vol. 4, 11th ed..

Eriksen, C. 2006. Kulturel mangfoldighed og menneskelig enhed. In *Wittgenstein om religion og religiøsitet*, ed. A.M. Christensen, 87–100. Aarhus: Aarhus University Press.

———. 2019. The Dynamics of Moral Revolutions – Prelude to Future Investigations and Interventions. *Ethical Theory and Moral Practice* 22 (3): 779–792.

———. Forthcoming. Contextual Ethics: Taking Lead from Løgstrup in Understanding Ethical Meaning and Normativity. *Sats - Nordic Journal of Philosophy, Special Issue on Contextual Ethics*. DOI: https://doi.org/10.1515/sats-2020-2009.

Fass, P.S. 2013. Is There a Story in the History of Childhood? In *The Routledge History of Childhood in the Western World*, ed. P.S. Fass. Oxon: Routledge.

Fenger, O. 1971. *Fejder og mandebod. Studier over slægstansvar i germansk og gammeldansk ret*. Copenhagen: Juristforbundets Forlag.

Fink, H. 2007. Om komplementariteten mellem den etiske fordring og alle personlige og sociale fordringer. In *Livtag med den etiske fordring*, ed. D. Bugge and P.A. Sørensen. Aarhus: Klim.

———. 2010. Efterskrift ved Hans Fink. In *Den Etiske Fordring*, ed. K.E. Løgstrup, 301–330. Aarhus: Klim.

———. 2012. Hvad er etik, egentlig? Elementer til en begrebsafklaring. In *Filosofi og etik*, ed. U. Thøgersen and B. Troelsen. Aalborg: Aalborg Universitetsforlag.

———. Forthcoming. Against Ethical Exceptionalism. *Sats - Nordic Journal of Philosophy, Special Issue on Contextual Ethics.*

Frankl, V.E. 2004. *Man's Search for Meaning*. London: Rider.

Freeman, M., ed. 2004. *Children's Rights*, Volume 1 + 2. The International Library of Essays on Rights. Hants: Dartmouth Publishing Company, Ashgate Publishing Limited.

———. 2012. Introduction. In *Law and Childhood Studies: Current Legal Issues*, ed. M. Freeman, vol. 14. Oxford: Oxford University Press.

Fuller, L.L. 1969. *The Morality of Law*. Revised ed. New Haven: Yale University Press.

Gardner, J. 2011. Some Types of Law. In *Common Law Theory*, ed. D.E. Edlin. New York: Cambridge University Press.

Grahn-Farley, M. 2013. *How Children Got Rights*. Dissertation, Harvard University, Harvard.

Green, L. 2013a. Should Law Improve Morality? *Criminal Law and Philosophy* 7: 473–494.

———. 2013b. The Morality in Law. *Oxford Legal Studies Research Paper*, 12.

Guenther, L. 2013. *Solitary Confinement – Social Death and Its Afterlives*. Minneapolis: University of Minneapolis Press.

Hacker, P.M.S. 1972. *Insight and Illusion: Wittgenstein on Philosophy and the Metaphysics of Experience*. Oxford: Oxford University Press.

———. 2015. Some Remarks on Philosophy and on Wittgenstein's Conception of Philosophy and Its Misinterpretation. *Argumenta: The Journal of the Italian Society for Analytic Philosophy* 1 (1): 43–59.

Hämäläinen, N. 2006. Finding a Place for Moral Theory. *Sats – Nordic Journal of Philosophy* 7 (2): 21–36.

———. 2016. *Descriptive Ethics – What Does Moral Philosophy Know about Morality?* New York: Palgrave Macmillan.

———. 2017. Three Metaphors towards a Conception of Moral Change. *Nordic Wittgenstein Review* 6 (2): 47–69.

Hanfling, O. 2003. Learning about Right and Wrong: Ethics and Language. *Philosophy* 78 (303): 25–41.

Harhoff, F. 1993. *Rigsfællesskabet*. Aarhus: Forlaget Klim.

Hart, H.L.A. 1997. *The Concept of Law*. 2nd ed. Oxford: Oxford University Press.

Haslanger, S. 2008. Changing the Ideology and Culture of Philosophy: Not By Reason (Alone). *Hypatia* 23 (2): 210–223.

Haug, M. C. 2017. Herman Cappelen, Tamar Szabó Gendler and John Hawthorne (Eds.). The Oxford Handbook of Philosophical Methodology. *Notre Dame Philosophical Reviews*, 23 January.

Held, V. 1990. Feminist Transformations of Moral Theory. *Philosophy and Phenomenological Research* 50 (Suppl): 321–344.

Heraclitus. 2003. *Fragments*. New York: Penguin Group.

Hermann, J. 2015. *On Moral Certainty, Justification and Practice: A Wittgensteinian Perspective*. New York: Palgrave Macmillan.

———. 2019. The Dynamics of Moral Progress. *Ratio* 32 (4): 300–311.

Heyes, C.J. 2003. Introduction. In *The Grammar of Politics: Wittgenstein and Political Philosophy*, ed. C.J. Heyes, 1–16. New York: Cornell University Press.

Hill, G. 1997. Solidarity, Objectivity, and the Human Form of Life: Wittgenstein vs. Rorty. *Critical Review* 11 (4): 555–580.

Hodges, M. 1995. The Status of Ethical Judgements in the Philosophical Investigations. *Philosophical Investigations* 18 (2): 99–112.

Högman. 2017. Angel Maker. http://www.hhogman.se/angel_maker.htm. Accessed 5 June 2017.

Holohan, A. 1987. Review: Debrah Dwork: War Is Good for Babies and Other Young Children. *Journal of Social Policy* 16: 582–584.

Holt, R. 1997. *Wittgenstein, Politics and Human Rights*. London: Routledge.

Hopf, T. 2018. Change in International Practices. *European Journal of International Relations* 24 (3): 687–711.

Hoy, D.C. 2005. *Critical Resistance: From Poststructuralism to Post-Critique*. Cambridge, MA: MIT Press.

Hunt, L. 2008. *Inventing Human Rights: A History*. New York: W. W. Norton & Company.

Hyman, J. 2015. *Action, Knowledge, & Will*. Oxford: Oxford University Press.

Ishay, M.R. 2008. *The History of Human Rights: From Ancient Times to the Globalization Era*. Berkeley: University of California Press.

Jaeggi, R. 2005. No Individual Can Resist: *Minima Moralia* as Critique of Forms of Life. *Constellations* 12 (1): 65–82.

———. 2018. *Critique of Forms of Life*. Cambridge, MA: The Belknap Press of Harvard University Press.

Jamieson, D. 2016. Slavery, Carbon, and Moral Progress. *Ethical Theory and Moral Practice* 20 (1): 169–184.

Jones, G. (Trans.). 2008. *Eirik the Red and Other Icelandic Sagas*. Oxford: Oxford University Press.

Keane, W. 2016a. *Ethical Life: Its Natural and Social Histories*. Princeton: Princeton University Press.

———. 2016b. An Interview with Webb Keane, Author of *Ethical Life: Its Natural and Social Histories*. http://blog.press.princeton.edu/2015/11/04/are-people-getting-better-an-interview-with-webb-keane-on-ethical-life/. Accessed 12 June 2017.

Kierkegaard, S. 1990. *Philosophiske Smuler*. Copenhagen: Hans Reitzels Forlag.

———. 1994a. *Synspunktet for min Forfatter-Virksomhed*. Copenhagen: Gyldendal.

———. 1994b. *Sygdom til Døden*. Copenhagen: Borgen.

———. 1996a. *Enten-Eller*. Bind 1 & 2. Copenhagen: Gyldendal.

———. 1996b. *Kjerlighedens Gjerninger*. Copenhagen: Gyldendal.

Kitcher, P. 2011. *The Ethical Project*. Cambridge, MA: Harvard University Press.

Koren, M. 1996. *Tell Me! The Right of the Child to Information*. Den Haag: NBLC Uitgeverij.

Krause, C., and M. Scheinen, eds. 2012. *International Protection of Human Rights: A Textbook*. Åbo: Åbo Akademi University.

Kuhn, T. 1970. *The Structure of Scientific Revolutions*. 2nd ed. Enlarged. Chicago: The University of Chicago Press.

Kuusela, O. 2008. *The Struggle Against Dogmatism: Wittgenstein and the Concept of Philosophy*. Cambridge, MA: Harvard University Press.

Laidlaw, J. 2011. Morality and Honour. *Anthropology of this Century*, 1. http://aotcpress.com/articles/morality-honour/. Accessed 12 March 2020.

Lambek, M. 2010. Introduction. In *Ordinary Ethics: Anthropology, Language, and Action*, ed. M. Lambek, 1–38. New York: Fordham University Press.

Lear, J. 1984. Moral Objectivity. *Royal Institute of Philosophy Lecture Series* 17: 135–170.

———. 2008. *Radical Hope: Ethics in the Face of Cultural Devastation*. Cambridge, MA: Harvard University Press.

———. 2011. *A Case for Irony*. Cambridge, MA: Harvard University Press.

Lewis, C.S. 2003. *The Lion, the Witch and the Wardrobe*. London: Collins.

Løgstrup, K.E. 1995. *Kunst og etik*. Copenhagen: Gyldendal.

———. 1997. *The Ethical Demand*. Notre Dame: University of Notre Dame Press.

———. 2020. *The Ethical Demand*. Oxford: Oxford University Press.

Lose, S. 2018. Røgfri fremtid kræver handling nu. *Jyllands-Posten* 1: 19.

Lov om ændring af lov om røgfri miljøer. 2012. Lov nr. 607 af 18/06/2012. https://www.retsinformation.dk/Forms/R0710.aspx?id=142456. Accessed 12 June 2017.

Lov om Røgfri Miljøer. 2007. Lov nr. 512 af 06/06/2007. https://www.retsinformation.dk/forms/r0710.aspx?id=11388. Accessed 12 June 2017.

Lovibond, S. 2019. Between Tradition and Criticism: The "Uncodifiability" of the normative. In *Ethics in the Wake of Wittgenstein*, ed. B. De Mesel and O. Kuusela, 84–102. Oxon: Routledge.

Macdonald, H. 2014. *H Is for Hawk*. London: Jonathan Cape.

Malacinski, L. 2011. Danskerne retter ind. *Jyllands-Posten* 1: 6–7.

Mandell, L. 2012. *Speaking Notes*. Prepared for the CLE Conference: Indigenous Legal Orders and the Common Law, November 15.

———. 2014. Telling a New Story: The William Decision. *Tsilhqot'in Nation v. British Columbia*, 2014 SCC 44. Speaking Notes.

———. 2015a. Speaking Notes and a Postscript Circling around the Open Field. Oktober 13.

———. 2015b. Speaking Notes for Gitxan Government Commission Community Meeting. January 19.

Mandell, L., and L. Pinder. 2012. Chapter Nine: Tracking Justice: The Constitution Express to Section 35 and Beyond. Draft.

Marks, S., and A. Clapham. 2005. Children. In *International Human Rights Lexicon*, ed. S. Marks and A. Clapham. Oxford: Oxford University Press.

Marmor, A. 2015. Introduction. In *The Routledge Companion to Philosophy of Law*, ed. A. Marmor, 3–16. New York: Routledge.

Marx, K., and F. Engels. 1888. *Manifesto of the Communist Party*. Reprint from the English edition of 1888, ed. F. Engels. Marston Gate: Amazon.co.uk, Ltd.

Mattingly, C. 2014. *Moral Laboratories. Family Peril and the Struggle for a Good Life*. Oakland: University of California Press.

Mayhew, J.H. 1967. Chimney-Sweepers. Crossing Sweepers. In *London Labour and the London Poor. A Cyclopaedia of the Conditions and Earnings of Those that Will Work, Those that Cannot Work, and Those that Will Not Work*, vol. 2, 338–465. London: Frank Cass & Co. Ltd.

McGillivray, A. 2011. Children's Rights, Paternal Power and Fiduciary Duty: From Roman Law to the Supreme Court of Canada. *International Journal of Children's Rights* 19: 21–54.

Minnameier, G. 2009. Measuring Moral Progress. A Neo-Kohlbergian Approach and Two Case Studies. *Journal of Adult Development* 16: 131–143.

MM/TF 2008: Mandag Morgen, Tryg Fonden. 2008. *Fremtidens forebyggelse – ifølge danskerne*. Copenhagen: Huset Mandag Morgen.

MM/TF 2017: Mandag Morgen, Tryg Fonden. 2017. *Mellem broccoli og bajere – forebyggelse ifølge danskerne*. Copenhagen: Huset Mandag Morgen.

Moeckli, D., S. Shah, and S. Sivakumaran, eds. 2014. *International Human Rights Law*. Oxford: Oxford University Press.

Moi, T. 2017. *Revolution of the Ordinary. Literary Studies after Wittgenstein, Austin, and Cavell*. Chicago: The University of Chicago Press.

Moody-Adams, M.M. 1999. The Idea of Moral Progress. *Metaphilosophy* 30 (3): 168–183.

———. 2002. *Fieldwork in Familiar Places: Morality, Culture and Philosophy*. Cambridge, MA: Harvard University Press.

———. 2017. Moral Progress and Human Agency. *Ethical Theory and Moral Practice* 20: 153–168.

Moore, M.J. 2010. Wittgenstein, Value Pluralism and Politics. *Philosophy and Social Criticism* 36 (9): 1113–1136.
Moore, M.S. 2012. The Various Relations between Law and Morality in Contemporary Legal Philosophy. *Ratio Juris* 25 (4): 435–471.
Morawetz, T. 2000a. The Concept of a Practice. In *Law's Premises, Law's Promise: Jurisprudence after Wittgenstein*, ed. T. Morawetz, 19–36. Burlington: Ashgate.
———. 2000b. Understanding, Disagreement and Conceptual Change. In *Law's Premises, Law's Promise: Jurisprudence after Wittgenstein*, ed. T. Morawetz, 37–54. Burlington: Ashgate.
Morrison, H., ed. 2012. *The Global History of Childhood Reader*. Oxon: Routledge.
Motzfeldt, H.M., and A. Næsborg-Andersen. 2018. Developing Administrative Law into Handling the Challenges of Digital Government in Denmark. *The Electronic Journal of e-Government* 16 (2): 136–146.
Moyal-Sharrock, D. 2015. Wittgenstein on Forms of Life, Patterns of Life and Ways of Living. *Nordic Wittgenstein Review* 4 (Special Issue): 21–42.
Musschenga, A.W., and G. Meynen. 2017. Moral Progress: An Introduction. *Ethical Theory and Moral Practice* 20 (1): 3–15.
Nehamas, A. 1994. *Life as Literature*. Cambridge: Harvard University Press.
Nickel, J.W. 2007. *Making Sense of Human Right*. Oxford: Blackwell Publishing.
Nickel, J. W. 2014. Human Rights. In *The Stanford Encyclopedia of Philosophy*, ed. E. N. Zalta, Spring 2014 ed. http://plato.stanford.edu/archives/spr2014/entries/rights-human/. Accessed 10 June 2017.
Nietzsche, F. 1993a. *Jenseits von Gut und Böse*. Berlin: Walter de Gruyter.
———. 1993b. *Zur Generalogie der Moral*. Berlin: Walter de Gruyter.
———. 1997. *Historiens nytte*. Copenhagen: Gyldendal.
———. 1999a. *Also Sprach Zarathustra*. Berlin: Walter de Gruyter.
———. 1999b. *Götzen-Dämmerung*. Berlin: Walter de Gruyter.
———. 1999c. *Ecce homo*. Berlin: Walter de Gruyter.
Nussbaum, M.C. 1998. Still Worthy of Praise. *Harvard Law Review* 111 (7): 1776–1795.
———. 2000. Why Practice Needs Ethical Theory: Particularism, Principle, and Bad Behaviour. In *Moral Particularism*, ed. B. Hooker and M.O. Little, 227–255. Oxford University Press.
———. 2001a. Introduction. In *Women, Culture, and Development*, ed. M.C. Nussbaum and J. Glover, 1–36. Oxford: Clarendon Press.
———. 2001b. Human Capabilities, Female Human Beings. In *Women, Culture, and Development*, ed. M.C. Nussbaum and J. Glover, 61–104. Oxford: Clarendon Press.
———. 2002. Non-Relative Virtues: An Aristotelian Approach. In *The Quality of Life*, ed. M.C. Nussbaum and A. Sen, 242–269. Oxford: Oxford University Press.
———. 2007. On Moral Progress: A Response to Richard Rorty. *The University of Chicago Law Review* 74 (3): 939–960.

———. 2011. *Creating Capabilities: The Human Development Approach*. Cambridge, MA: The Belknap Press of Harvard University Press.

Nussbaum, M. C. 2016. Beyond Anger. https://aeon.co/essays/there-s-no-emotion-we-ought-to-think-harder-about-than-anger. Accessed 12 April 2017.

Nussbaum, M.C. 2019. *The Monarchy of Fear*. New York: Simon & Schuster Paperbacks.

Nussbaum, M.C., and A. Sen. 2002. Introduction. In *The Quality of Life*, ed. M.C. Nussbaum and A. Sen, 1–8. Oxford: Oxford University Press.

O'Hara, N. 2018. *Moral Certainty and the Foundations of Morality*. New York: Palgrave Macmillan.

Orange, T. 2018. *There There*. London: Harvill Secker.

Orsi, R.A. 2016. *History and Presence*. Cambridge, MA: The Belknap Press of Harvard University Press.

Oshatz, M. 2008. The Problem of Moral Progress: The Slavery Debates and Development of Liberal Protestantism in the United States. *Modern Intellectual History* 5: 225–250.

Palmer, D., and M. Schagrin. 1978. Moral Revolutions. *Philosophy and Phenomenological Research* 39 (2): 262–273.

Patterson, D.M. 1990. Law's Pragmatism: Law as Practice & Narrative. *Virginia Law Review* 76: 937–996.

———. 2010. Introduction. In *A Companion to Philosophy of Law and Legal Theory*, ed. D. Patterson, 2nd ed. Oxford: Wiley-Blackwell.

Pauer-Studer, H., and D.J. Velleman. 2011. Distortions of Normativity. *Ethical Theory and Moral Practice* 14: 329–356.

Phillips, D.Z. 1993. Authorship and Authenticity: Kierkegaard and Wittgenstein. In *Wittgenstein and Religion*, ed. D.Z. Phillips. Houndmills, Basingstoke: Macmillan.

Pitt, J. 2001. The Dilemma of Case Studies: Toward a Heraclitian Philosophy of Science. *Perspectives on Science* 9 (4): 373–382.

Pleasants, N.J. 2008. Wittgenstein, Ethics and Basic Moral Certainty. *Inquiry* 51 (3): 241–267.

———. 2000. Winch, Wittgenstein and the Idea of a Critical Social Theory. *History of the Social Sciences* 13 (1): 78–91.

———. 2018. The Structure of Moral Revolutions. *Social Theory and Practice* 44 (4): 567–592.

Posner, R.A. 1998a. The Problematics of Moral and Legal Theory. *Harvard Law Review* 111: 1637–1717.

———. 1998b. Reply to Critics of the Problematics of Moral and Legal Theory. *Harvard Law Review* 111: 1796–1823.

Prichard, D. 2012. Wittgenstein and the Groundlessness of Our Believing. *Synthese* 189: 255–272.

Radbruch, G. 1961a. Erste Stellungnahme nach dem Zusammenbruch 1945. In *Der Mensch im Recht: Ausgewählte Vorträge und Aufsätze über Grundfragen des Rechts*, ed. G. Radbruch. Göttingen: Vandenhoeck & Ruprecht.

———. 1961b. Gesetzliches Unrecht und übergesetzliches Recht. In *Der Mensch im Recht: Ausgewählte Vorträge und Aufsätze über Grundfragen des Rechts*, ed. G. Radbruch. Göttingen: Vandenhoeck & Ruprecht.

Raz, J. 1994. Moral Change and Social Relativism. *Social Philosophy and Policy* 11 (1): 139–158.

Read, R. 2016. Wittgenstein and the Illusion of 'Progress': On Real Politics and Real Philosophy in a World of Technocracy. *Royal Institute of Philosophy Supplement* 78: 265–284.

Robbins, J. 2004. *Becoming Sinners*. Berkeley: University of California Press.

———. 2007. Between Reproduction and Freedom: Morality, Value, and Radical Cultural Change. *Ethnos* 72 (3): 293–314.

———. 2016. What Is the Matter with Transcendence? On the Place of Religion in the New Anthropology of Ethics. *Journal of the Royal Anthropological Institute* 22 (4): 781–785.

Rønnow-Rasmussen, T. 2017. On Locating Value in Making Moral Progress. *Ethical Theory and Moral Practice* 20 (1): 137–152.

Rorty, R. 1989. *Contingency, Irony and Solidarity*. Cambridge: Cambridge University Press.

———. 1999. *Philosophy and Social Hope*. London: Penguin Books.

———. 2007. Dewey and Posner and Moral Progress. *The University of Chicago Law Review* 74 (3): 915–927.

Roth, A. 2012. Ethical Progress as Problem-Resolving. *The Journal of Political Philosophy* 20 (4): 384–406.

Schiller, N.G. 2016. Positioning Theory: An Introduction. *Anthropological Theory* 16 (2–3): 133–145.

Sen, A. 2007. *Identity and Violence: The Illusion of Destiny*. New York: W. W. Norton & Company.

Singer, P. 2008. Is There Moral Progress? https://www.project-syndicate.org/commentary/is-there-moral-progress?barrier=accessreg. Accessed 8 June 2017.

Sophocles. 2003. *Antigone*. Cambridge: Cambridge University Press.

Stearns, P.N. 2006. *Childhood in World History*. New York: Routledge.

Stephens, S. 2012. Children and the Politics of Culture in 'Late Capitalism'. In *The Global History of Childhood Reader*, ed. H. Morrison, 375–393. Oxon: Routledge.

Stern, D.G. 2003. The Practical Turn. In *The Blackwell Guide to the Philosophy of the Social Sciences*, ed. S.P. Turner and P.A. Roth, 185–206. Oxford: Blackwell Publishing.

Summers, J.S. 2016. Rationalizing Our Way into Moral Progress. *Ethical Theory and Moral Practice* 20 (1): 93–104.

Sunstein, C. 2019. *How Change Happens.* Cambridge, MA: The MIT Press.

Tully, J. 2003. Wittgenstein and Political Philosophy: Understanding Practices of Critical Reflection. In *The Grammar of Politics: Wittgenstein and Political Philosophy*, ed. C. Heyes, 17–42. New York: Cornell University Press.

Tumulty, P. 2009. Recognizing Varieties of Objectivity in Promoting a Global Culture of Human Rights: Remarks on the Tradition of Plato, Kierkegaard and Wittgenstein. *International Philosophical Quarterly* 49 (4): 473–483.

United Nations. 1924. *Geneva Declaration of the Rights of the Child. League of Nations.* http://www.un-documents.net/gdrc1924.htm. Accessed 12 June 2017.

———. n.d. *United Nations Declaration on the Rights of Indigenous Peoples.* https://www.un.org/development/desa/indigenouspeoples/declaration-on-the-rights-of-indigenous-peoples.html. Accessed 12 June 2017.

United Nations, Office of the High Commissioner for Human Rights. 2007. *Legislative History of the Convention on the Rights of the Child.* Vol. 1. New York: United Nations.

Universal Declaration of Human Rights, G.A. Res. 217A (III), U.N. Doc. A/810 at 71. 1948.

Van Buren, G. 1995. *The International Law of the Rights of the Child.* Leiden: Martinus Nijhoff Publishers.

Van der Burg, W. 2003. Dynamic Ethics. *The Journal of Value Inquiry* 37: 13–34.

———. 2014. *The Dynamics of Law and Morality. A Pluralist Account of Legal Interactionism.* Surrey: Ashgate.

Vattimo, G. 2005. *Nihilisme og emancipation – etik, politik, ret.* Aarhus: Aarhus Universitetsforlag.

Vial-Dumas, M. 2014. Parents, Children, and Law: *Patria Potestas* and Emancipation in the Christian Mediterranean during Late Antiquity and the Early Middle Ages. *Journal of Family History* 39 (4): 307–329.

Viskum, B. 2015. In the Name of the Law: How Consistency Can Enhance Legal Legitimacy. In *Law & Legitimacy*, ed. P. Andersen, C. Eriksen, and B. Viskum, 57–72. Copenhagen: Djøf Forlag.

Von Wright, G.H. 1994. *Myten om Fremskridtet: Tanker 1987–92 med en intellektuel selvbiografi.* Copenhagen: Munksgaard/Rosinante.

Waldenfels, B. 2011a. In Place of the Other. *Continental Philosophical Review* 44 (2): 151–164.

———. 2011b. *Phenomenology of the Alien.* Evanston: Northwestern University Press.

Waldron, H.A. 1983. A Brief History of Scrotal Cancer. *British Journal of Industrial Medicine* 40 (4): 390–401.

Weber, M. 2009. *Den protestantiske etik og kapitalismens ånd.* Copenhagen: Nansensgade Antikvariat.

Weston, M. 1999. Evading the Issue: The Strategy of Kierkegaard's Postscript. *Philosophical Investigations* 22 (1): 35–64.

Widlok, T. 2013. Norm and Spontaneity. Elicitation with Moral Dilemma Scenarios. In *The Anthropology of Moralities*, ed. M. Heintz, 20–47. New York: Berghahn Books.

Williams, M. 1999. *Wittgenstein, Mind and Meaning: Towards a Social Conception of Mind*. New York: Routledge.

———. 2009. Normative Naturalism. *International Journal of Philosophical Studies* 18 (3): 355–375.

Williams, B. 2011. *Ethics and the Limits of Philosophy*. Oxon: Routledge.

Wilson, C. 2010. Moral Progress Without Moral Realism. *Philosophical Papers* 39 (1): 97–116.

Winch, P. 2008. *The Idea of a Social Science and its Relation to Philosophy*. Oxon: Routledge.

Wittgenstein, L. 1993a. Remarks on Frazer's *Golden Bough*. In *Philosophical Occasions 1912–1951*, ed. J. Klagge and A. Nordmann, 119–155. Indianapolis: Hackett Publishing Company.

———. 1993b. A Lecture on Ethics. In *Philosophical Occasions 1912–1951*, ed. J. Klagge and A. Nordmann. Indianapolis: Hackett Publishing Company.

———. 1995. *Cambridge Letters. Correspondence with Russell, Keynes, Moore, Ramsey and Sraffa*. Oxford: Blackwell.

———. 1997. *Lectures and Conversations on Aesthetics, Psychology and Religious Belief.* Oxford: Basil Blackwell.

———. 2001. *Remarks on the Foundations of Mathematics*. Oxford: Basil Blackwell.

———. 2004. *Zettel*. Oxford: Blackwell Publishing.

———. 2006. *Culture and Value*. Oxford: Blackwell Publishing.

———. 2009. *Philosophische Untersuchungen*. Ed. P. Hacker and J. Schulte. West Sussex: Wiley-Blackwell.

———. 2016. *On Certainty*. Oxford: Blackwell Publishing.

Wolcher, L.E. 2012. The Ethics of the Unsaid in the Sphere of Human Rights. *Notre Dame Journal of Law, Ethics & Public Policy* 26 (2): 533–547.

Zigon, J. 2013. Human Rights as Moral Progress? A Critique. *Cultural Anthropology* 28 (4): 716–736.

———. 2014. An Ethics of Dwelling and a Politics of World-Building: A Critical Response to Ordinary Ethics. *Journal of the Royal Anthropological Institute* 20 (4): 746–764.

———. 2019. *A War on People: Drug User Politics and a New Ethics of Community*. Oakland: University of California Press.

# Index[1]



[1] Note: Page numbers followed by 'n' refer to notes.


C. Eriksen, *Moral Change*,
https://doi.org/10.1007/978-3-030-61037-1

The manufacturer's authorised representative in the EU is Springer Nature Customer Service Centre GmbH, Europaplatz 3, 69115 Heidelberg, Germany. If you have any concerns regarding our products, please contact ProductSafety@springernature.com

Printed and bound by CPI Group (UK) Ltd, Croydon, CR0 4YY
30/09/2026
02225451-0001